DATE DUE

THE CHURCH

offensive, uncomfortable, unstoppable

CHURCH
THE

WHAT WE ARE MEANT TO BE

KEN HUTCHERSON

Multnomah Books *Sisters, Oregon*

THE CHURCH
published by Multnomah Publishers, Inc.

International Standard Book Number: 1-57673-253-3

Cover photograph by Bill Cannon

Unless otherwise noted, Scripture quotations are from
The New Scofield Study Bible, King James Version © 1967 by Oxford University Press, Inc.
Used by permission.

Other Scripture quotations are from
New American Standard Bible (NASB) © 1960, 1977 by the Lockman Foundation
The Holy Bible, New International Version (NIV) © 1973, 1984 by International Bible
Society, used by permission of Zondervan Publishing House
The Holy Bible, New King James Version (NKJV) © 1984 by Thomas Nelson, Inc.
Used by permission.
The New Testament in Modern English, Revised Edition (Phillips) © 1972 by J. B. Phillips

For information:
Multnomah Publishers, Inc.•Post Office Box 1720•Sisters, Oregon 97759

Library of Congress Cataloging-in-Publication Data:
Hutcherson, Ken.
  The church / by Ken Hutcherson.
    p. cm.
  ISBN 1–57673–253–3 (paper)
  1. Church—Biblical teaching. 2. Bible. N.T.—Criticism, interpretation, etc.
  3. Bible. N.T. Acts—Criticism, interpretation, etc. I. Title.
BS2545.C5H87   1998
262–dc21   97–49257
                                                                       CIP

98 99 00 01 02 03 04 05 — 10 9 8 7 6 5 4 3 2 1

*I would like to dedicate this book to my wife, Pat.
She has stood beside me and encouraged me
to stand behind the black and white issues of Scripture—even
when it hasn't been popular.*

*By far, the best dedication anyone can have
is to live a righteous life before Jesus Christ.*

CONTENTS

So tell us, Hutch…
why has the church become so weak and anemic today?

FOREWORD

Let me get to the point. This is a great book. Because its point is great. And its author will grab your heart.

This is a book about Jesus' dream. Everyone seems to be asking, *What Would Jesus Do?* As if there was any doubt! The one thing Jesus was always doing was building His church. No doubt about it, it's still the one thing that interests Him the most. "I will build My church!" Those five little monosyllabic words that Jesus so emphatically pronounced changed the course of history.

Ken Hutcherson has caught that vision. More accurately, Jesus' vision has caught Ken Hutcherson! That "caught vision" is changing lives in greater Seattle. And if it catches you, my friend, it will go far deeper than a bracelet on your wrist. You will develop a heart after Christ's and eyes for His kingdom.

Ken's vision for the church is deep and personal. And it manifests itself *locally*, far beyond some vague concept of a "universal church" that has never yet held a meeting. After all, the church Jesus was interested in building was the one where people live. Where YOU live! The New Testament is not so much about the universal church as it is about the church in Jerusalem...and Antioch...and Ephesus...and Thessalonica...and Philippi...and out to men and women in communities on the very edges of that day's known world. As far as I can tell, the Holy Spirit never once inspired an epistle to "the universal church." But He did write extensively and passionately to local churches—churches made up of local people with local leaders and local influence, living in a local community. Those inspired letters are full of principles intended to be easily transferable to other local churches.

Ken Hutcherson pastors a local church with all the heart—

and color—of the New Testament. In that kind of church people love each other so obviously that the world must know that the Father sent the Son…and that "something supernatural is going on here." As the walls come down, the name of Christ is lifted up.

Speaking of those walls…when I was a little boy I was struck by Norman Rockwell's picture of the little black girl, escorted by federal marshals, trying to walk to school at Little Rock's Central High. An ugly crowd threw tomatoes—red missiles of hate that stained the wall next to her. I remember my childhood anger at such injustice. And I remember my childhood prayer that God would give me a black friend so we could become bosom buddies, play ball on the same teams, whip the world in athletic competition (and everything else that came along), and in the process, display a brotherly bond so deep no one would ever again accept racism.

God never answered that prayer…or so I thought for a long time.

Several decades later that prayer came to mind as I sat across my kitchen table from Hutch. Ken Hutcherson, my dear friend and fellow pastor, grew up in Alabama with a hatred for whites that dominated his outlook on everything in life, including athletics. Hutch was blessed with a big body and enormous muscular power. His primary events on the track team give you a clue. He ran the 100, 220, and threw the shotput. He also played football…because that was a way he could "hurt whites legally." Ken's abilities took him to the highest levels of the sport. As a professional, he played linebacker for the Dallas Cowboys and Seattle Seahawks, until he blew out his knee.

But in God's providence, that career-ending injury became a church-launching opportunity!

You see, somewhere along the line Hutch fell in love with

Jesus Christ. And if you love Jesus, you're going to love His church! It makes a certain amount of sense: you can't walk with Christ if you don't walk with His Body. With all the fervor of a linebacker, Hutch became a student of the Book. And a churchman. Eventually he became a pastor, leading a truly multicultural church of several thousand people in east Seattle. Does God have a sense of humor or what? The walls are coming down...the church is growing up...and Jesus' dream is being fulfilled.

My childhood prayer for a ball-playing friend took a twist I didn't anticipate at the time. But I have the honor of calling Hutch my friend, and we're having a ball involved with Jesus in building His church. You ought to come along. Indeed, if you'll allow the burden of this book (not to mention the Bible) to capture your heart, you will become involved in the greatest movement and family in the history of the earth. The church. *His* church.

Like the Lord he loves, Ken is "full of grace and truth." And humor! Delightfully hilarious, appropriately serious, and always faithful to God's Word, Hutch will turn your heart toward the Lord...and His church. You will smile, laugh, cry (squirm), and sit up and take notice. And if you're not careful, you will become a churchman...doing what Jesus would do. There's no doubt about it.

Stu Weber
Gresham, Oregon
1998

SOME OPENING THOUGHTS

Modern conveniences make life just a little easier. But after a while, we can get so used to the "conveniences" we begin to think they're necessities. We begin to think we can't live without them.

For instance, it's pretty tough to think about trying to get along without a car. When you think about it, we've had cars in our world for less than a hundred years. And all that time before cars were invented, people somehow managed to get by.

But now...how could I live without my beautiful, black Dodge Ram 2500 Cummins diesel pickup? Yes, I know the wheels on the city bus go round and round...but man! I don't want to be cooling my heels at some bus stop on a rainy street in Seattle. I want my truck! I like my truck. Don't touch my truck!

It gets worse.

Now it's not good enough to have just one set of wheels. The family is deprived if you don't have two—or three. You know, it's just so inconvenient to have one car. It's a hardship!

And it isn't only cars. We become so used to our little time-saving, labor-saving devices and gadgets that we feel seriously abused when we have to resort to doing something manually. What do kids complain about today? Loading the dishwasher! Can you believe it? That just doesn't compute!

"Load that dishwasher."

"I don't want to load the dishwasher."

You can easily take care of that situation; just lock the sucker up for three months and let 'im bust suds! Within a few days he'll be begging you, "Please, let me load the dishwasher! I like to load the dishwasher! I love that dishwasher."

I guess I shouldn't get on the kids too much, because I've got my own favorite gadgets. Have you ever used one of those new sonic toothbrushes? It uses sound waves to shine up your teeth. You see, I've got one. That's why I've got such a beautiful smile.

As with a lot of these high-tech contraptions, they tell you to always read the instructions before plugging it in and turning it on. But I thought, *An instruction manual for a toothbrush? Naw!*

That was my thought before I turned it on.

If I'd read the instruction manual, I would have known that you're supposed to turn it off before you take it out of your mouth. Because if you don't, it will give your lips exercise they've never had before. Besides that, toothpaste and whatever else is mixed in will just explode all over the place. And suddenly the bathroom mirror is looking pretty bad and you have to clean it up before your wife walks in.

What if the Lord didn't intend us to be comfortable?

The other day while I was zapping my teeth the thing slipped out of my hand. There used to be a time when your hand stopped the toothbrush stopped, too. Not today! My hand slipped off, so I made a grab at the toothbrush to get it back in my mouth. Man, that thing beat me so hard across the lips and gums I couldn't brush my teeth for three days.

Another time I was in the middle of my oral hygiene and the toothbrush just quit on me. Suddenly the thing went dead. For a moment I caught myself thinking, *Man, what am I going to do? I can't finish brushing my teeth! I don't have time to charge this thing up before I can finish my teeth!* About that time my brain kicked in and said, "Move your hand, dummy, it still has a brush on the end."

Oh yeah.

You know how it is. You just get so used to the way things are now that you imagine it's always been that way and that you can't live without those things. Have you ever thought about that? Sometimes God has to come along and remove something from our lives to show us that it wasn't really as important or necessary as we thought it was. But it's hard to change! It's hard to let go of a tradition or a practice or something we've become accustomed to.

I believe that's the way it is in the church today.

We have our practices and our traditions, our customs and our attitudes. And we're comfortable with those. They fit nice and easy, like an old slipper.

But hear me, please.

What if the Lord of the church didn't intend us to be comfortable and easy?

What if we discover the Word of God says something about the church that's different than we learned or expected or remembered? What if His words are uncomfortable and challenge some of our well-worn routines and habits? What then?

We look at different churches today, and they look about the way we expect them to look. To our eyes, they look "normal." We assume—just because it's always been a certain way ever since we can remember—that everything is operating according to God's plan. That's a dangerous assumption! Our eyes may not be seeing things the same way God's eyes see things.

When the Lord Jesus confronted the seven churches in the book of Revelation, He reminded them, "These things saith the Son of God, who hath his eyes like unto a flame of fire" (Revelation 2:18).

The more time we spend in the Instruction Manual, learning what the New Testament church really looks like from the Lord's point of view, the more we begin to wonder how we've drifted so far from the original design. If we stay away from the Instruction Manual we might think we're doing pretty well. We see church growth and people being saved (a few, anyway), and we figure God's got to be pleased.

But is He? What pleases God?

Obedience pleases God. God is pleased when the church lines up with His instructions in His Word.

For instance: I see an all-white church on one side of town. I see an all-black church on the other side of town. I see Hispanic churches and Korean churches and Chinese churches. And some of these fellowships of believers are excited and growing like crazy. But it's strange...I can't find anywhere in the Instruction Manual that says Christ's church is supposed to be racially or culturally divided in that way.

Is God pleased?

God tells us, "I've given instructions; I've started a new thing in the book of Acts, and this is what the New Testament church should look like."

But if I don't read the Instruction Manual, if I don't study what the newborn church looked like in the book of Acts, I imagine things are just fine.

It's the same thing with a marriage relationship. If I don't know and understand what God has said about marriage and the responsibilities of a husband and wife, I can have a dangerously sick marriage and not really know it. How many people have come home in the evening only to find their spouse has packed up and gone? And they thought their marriage had been "just fine."

If you're not reading the Instruction Manual you may be in trouble. You may be walking close to the edge in many areas of life and not even be aware of it. How many times do you read about a teen committing a rape or doing drugs or taking his or her own life and the parents are shell-shocked? They say, "We don't get it. Everything seemed just fine. Everything seemed normal."

But things weren't normal at all. Because if we're only comparing ourselves with our neighbors and with our culture, we'll have a skewed, distorted point of view. The Word of God is the standard.

That's pretty much the same thing Paul told the Corinthians, after they'd caught the "comparison disease."

> For we dare not class ourselves or compare ourselves with those who commend themselves. But they, measuring themselves by themselves, and comparing themselves among themselves, are not wise (2 Corinthians 10:12, NKJV).

If you're just comparing yourself to people you know, you may think you're a great parent or a good husband or wife. But the next thing you know, the bottom falls out of what looked like a solid marriage or family.

And you're surprised...because you didn't read the Manual.

That's the reason we began Antioch Bible Church.

And that's the reason I've written this book.

I've studied the Manual, and I'm concerned about what I see in today's church. You may be saying, "Oh, that Hutch, he's just stuck-up and stuck on his own narrow opinions. He thinks he's the only one with the message."

No, I'm not saying that at all. I'm just saying I've walked back and forth through the pages of the book of Acts, and I've come to the conclusion that we might be a lot more comfortable and easy than we ought to be. We may be walking close to some dangerous cliff edges and not even be aware of it.

Maybe we're not supposed to be quite so comfortable.

Maybe we're not supposed to be quite so easy and relaxed.

Maybe the Bible has some things to say about our church that we don't really want to hear.

I've talked to a number of people who've seen some of the same things I've seen in God's Word…but don't want to do anything about it. I've talked with pastors who tend to agree with me but say, "If I made some of the changes you're talking about, the congregation would come unglued. Our leadership would fire me so fast it would make your head spin. We have people who would go nuts if we tried to do things like that."

Do we really want to do it God's way?

I'm not afraid of losing my job, because Antioch Bible Church doesn't hold my job. Antioch is where I've been called to minister, but it's not my job. My job is to be right before God. And He knows how to take care of old Hutch.

As you read this book, you may feel I'm getting too personal with some of the verses I'll be dealing with. You may feel your toes being stepped on.

Stepping on toes really isn't one of my purposes. I have better things to do; you'll just have to take my word for that. On the other hand, if the teaching of the Word of God steps on your toes, you might need to ask yourself: What am I doing with my feet in the wrong place? If you are offended by the plain teaching of the Word of God, that means you need to get your life turned around.

If you're offended by *me*, of course, that's another issue. I'm an old NFL linebacker, and they used to pay me to get in people's faces. If you don't like that up-close-and-personal style of teaching, you can deal with that however you want to; it won't hurt my feelings. Linebackers are used to be being shoved back and rejected. But if the Word of God deals with you, you have only one thing to do…and that is to make sure your life lines up with what God has spoken.

Simply put, the purpose of the church is to teach the Word of God. And when the Word of God gets on your case and you find yourself taking it personally, it might mean God wants something to change in your life.

Now the question that we should ask ourselves every day, every moment of our lives is, Do I really want to do it God's way? That's a good, penetrating question. It can cause you a lot of discomfort. Even a little pain. It can also bring you more joy than you've experienced since that first day when you said "yes" to Jesus Christ.

"Yes, Lord," are very good words.

I don't know of any better.

THE CHURCH

BECAUSE WE AREN'T FILLED WITH THE SPIRIT

W hat Jesus promised in the last verses of Luke's gospel, He delivered in the second chapter of Acts.

And behold, I send the promise of my Father upon you; but tarry ye in the city of Jerusalem until ye be endued with power from on high (Luke 24:49).

"Power from on high." On the day of Pentecost, the power of God entered the church through the permanent giving of the Holy Spirit.

Power from on high.

Where has that power gone in today's church?

When the Holy Spirit came at Pentecost, it wasn't dynamite, it was a dynamo! Dynamite makes a loud noise, kicks up a lot of dust, and it's over. A dynamo is a continual source of power. It builds and builds and builds, and the power never stops flowing.

In other words, the book of Acts is more than ancient history. In one sense, it is never finished because you and I continue the acts of the Holy Spirit in the church of Jesus Christ today.

Here's what amazes me about Pentecost. Think about it. What did they do? They prayed for thirty days, then preached for thirty minutes, and three thousand people were added to the church immediately.

Three thousand in one day, one service! So what do we do when we want to see God move? We pray for thirty minutes, preach three thousand sermons, have thirty people saved, and shout, "Yes! Pentecost all over again!"

Something is missing.

Some*one* is missing.

Christians on all sides of us are living defeated lives because they're not experiencing the filling and the control of the Holy Spirit. It's amazing! You look around and see Christians with longer faces than nonbelievers ever thought of having. Why? Because deep down, those children of God know something isn't right. Something (Someone) keeps whispering that life isn't what it could be…would be…should be…if they were walking in fellowship with the Spirit. A Christian who is living outside the control of the Holy Spirit is the most miserable person in the world. A nonbeliever realizes he isn't happy or complete, but thinks that's just the natural state of things; he really doesn't expect life to be much different. But a believer in Jesus Christ *knows* when his life isn't measuring up. To use the picture Jesus used in Revelation 2:5, he knows the heights from which he has fallen.

Our very lives are a book of Acts. With each passing day, the Holy Spirit is writing new chapters as you and I are squeezed, molded, pressed, hammered, and slowly transformed into the image of God's Son.

At least…that's what the Spirit *wants* to do in your life.

But many of us aren't on speaking terms with Him.

WAIT TRAINING

Jesus had just finished ascending into heaven, and the disciples were standing there on the dusty outskirts of Bethany with heads tilted back and mouths hanging open.

Whoosh!

It's not every day you see someone take off like that—and this was quite a few years before the Wright brothers. The disciples watched Him shoot up into the atmosphere and grow smaller and smaller in that big blue sky until He was just a dot, and then they couldn't see Him anymore. But even after He disappeared, no one wanted to move. They were still staring.

After all the great, amazing events… God was telling them to wait.

The Lord was gone! Really, really gone. What were they going to do?

They might still be standing there if a couple of angels hadn't come along and said, "C'mon, guys. Back down to earth! It's time to move on. Don't just stand around looking. He's going to come back just the way He went (whoosh!), and when He comes, you'd better make sure He doesn't catch you looking!"

That got them moving. "Oh yeah! He told us to go to Jerusalem and do something, didn't He? Guess we best get our feet moving."

> Then returned they unto Jerusalem from the mount called Olivet, which is from Jerusalem a sabbath day's journey. And when they were come in, they went up into an upper room where abode Peter, and James, and John, and Andrew, Philip, and Thomas, Bartholomew, and Matthew, James, the son of Alphaeus, and Simon the Zealot, and Judas, the son of James. These all continued with one accord in prayer and supplication, with the women, and Mary, the mother of Jesus, and with his brethren (Acts 1:12–14).

With Jesus ascended into heaven, there wasn't much to do but obey. They gathered together in that room and prayed and waited for the promised "power from on high" (whatever that was).

The Lord had said, I'm going to send you the Holy Spirit and that Holy Spirit is *power.* I'm going to send you what is equivalent to an atomic bomb—so much power by My Spirit you aren't going to be able to contain it when it gets here.

That was the promise. But what was the first thing they had to do after they watched Him ascend into that blue Judean sky?

They had to wait.

Can you believe it? After all the promises, after all the miracles, after all the great, amazing events, God was telling them to get together in a room and wait patiently for what He was going to do next.

I believe this is something of a picture for you and me, a pattern that the Lord establishes in this important transitional book of Acts. There's something in the unfolding of all this that tells us how grace is going to work in our lives.

Going back to that upper room must have been tough. The disciples had just seen Jesus return to heaven to take His seat at the Father's right hand. This was their Lord, triumphant over death and hell! I can imagine they must have been just a little bit excited here. I can imagine them saying, "C'mon, guys, we've heard the promises, we've seen Jesus taken to heaven in triumph. He told us we'd be clothed with power. He told us we'd be His witnesses through the whole world. Let's get after it! Let's go take over the world for Jesus!"

God doesn't seem to be in the habit of laying down time limits.

But their Lord had said, "You go wait."

Waiting is not an American characteristic. It's never been one of my strengths, either. Why is it so hard to wait?

You and I find ourselves in certain predicaments and we think we have the right to tell God, "I've waited long enough." Maybe you have a situation in your marriage that's driving you crazy. You have a mate who's gone haywire, whoop-de-whoops, out there in the ozone somewhere, doing crazy stuff. What could be more stressful than that? And you've prayed and prayed and waited and waited for God to work. You've waited for thirty minutes, or thirty days—or even thirty years. And now you're telling God, "Enough of this! I'm tired. I don't think it's fair for me to have to wait any longer."

It's an interesting thing: I've read my Bible through and through, and whenever God asks you and me to wait, He doesn't seem to be in the habit of laying down time limits. He doesn't say, "Wait two days, or wait two weeks, or wait two years." That would be easier, wouldn't it? We could have it on our calendar: "God's going to do thus and so at 2:00 P.M., Pacific Standard Time, on February 7, 2002," and just scratch off the days one by one until the time came.

But that wouldn't do much for our faith, would it? Instead of waiting on *Him* day by day, we'd be waiting on a certain day or hour. At the beginning of this first chapter of Acts, that's exactly what the disciples wanted. A timetable!

> When they therefore were come together, they asked of him, saying, Lord, wilt thou at this time restore again the kingdom to Israel? (1:6)

And what did they get for that question? They got a rebuke, that's what they got! And that rebuke—followed again by a promise!—was one of the last things Jesus said to them:

> It is not for you to know the times or the seasons, which the Father hath put in his own power. But ye shall receive power, after that the Holy Spirit is come upon you... (1:7–8).

It had seemed very logical to the disciples that the Lord should establish His "new world order" right then. What could be better than NOW?

Isn't that like us? "Lord, I've prayed. I've waited. I've done my duty. If You're ever going to answer, today would be an ideal time, don't You think?"

Can you imagine the disciples saying, "All right now, do You want this to work or not, God? You'd better get that Holy Spirit down here *fast*. We're getting out of this upper room. We're getting claustrophobia. It's getting kind of sweaty in here, and everyone's just a little uptight. It won't be long before we're fightin' and fussin'. We need that permanent giving of the Holy Spirit right now so we can work together!"

He asked them to wait for *His* timing.

When I think about waiting for God's best, I'm reminded of the way my wife, Pat, came into my life. After retiring from football and plunging into the ministry, I had a strong reluctance to allow anything or anyone to come between me and what God had called me to do. I knew that God's priorities for a married man are: God, family, and ministry (or, if you're not in full-time ministry, God, family, job, ministry).

People kept saying to me, "Man, you're not getting any younger. You'd better get married. You've had a lot going for you, professional football, the ministry…but it's time you established a home!" If they'd been even more honest with me, they might have said, "Hutch, your life is out of balance. You're speaking all the time, teaching all the time, traveling all the time—you're running yourself ragged. You're out in the ozone, man."

I was dating, but somehow I never seemed to meet "the right one." Pat was working with me in high school ministry at that time, and I couldn't help but be impressed by her qualities. As I dated, I kept comparing the different girls to Pat—their commitment, their personalities, their desire to please God—and they all fell short by comparison. Then one day it hit me. *Why am I comparing all the girls with her? There she is right in front of me!*

Because I waited, God gave me the perfect mate for the ministry that I have. She complements everything I do and keeps me from getting overcommitted, underrested, and out of healthy balance. I love my life now, and ministry has never been more fulfilling. How glad I am that I waited for God's best!

WHAT TO DO WHILE YOU'RE WAITING

These all continued with one accord in prayer and supplication.…

What were they doing while they waited for the promise of the Spirit? Counting flowers on the wall? Playing Solitaire? Watching videos? Twiddling their thumbs? No, they weren't "just waiting." They were waiting on the Lord.

It isn't enough just to wait, you've got to wait *right*. This wasn't a bus they were waiting for, they were waiting on the living God! This is the true wait-control program! Now, perhaps you've found yourself waiting for your spouse to change, or for a ministry, or for God to move in a particular situation in your life. What is your attitude while you're waiting? So many times our attitude just stinks! And the waiting time becomes wasted time.

It isn't enough just to wait, you've got to wait right.

"Oh my, oh me!" we say. "Here I am, poor me, waiting and waiting so patiently (ha!) for the Lord to work. I'm just suffering for Jesus." But all the while, you haven't been praying, you haven't been seeking God's face, you've just been marking time—and passing along your rotten attitude to others! That is *not* waiting on the Lord, and that brand of waiting doesn't mean a hill of beans to God.

You've got to wait right.

And that means without complaints. Without contempt for others. It means waiting with peace, waiting with love, and waiting with hope…clinging to your faith in a God who loves you and desires your best.

We're so impatient. We look at our employer, who's giving us ulcers, and we say, "I've waited and waited and I've just about had it. Heaven and earth may pass away, but that old dog is *never* going to change."

And we think God's going to bless that kind of attitude? Those folks in the upper room waited in prayer and supplication. They took it all before the Lord: their doubts, their fears, their sorrows, their hopes, and their longings. The waiting wasn't wasted time at all; they were drawing near to God—and drawing near to each other at the same time.

The easiest thing to do without Him is nothing at all.

Here's one of Hutch's bottom lines, take it or leave it: If you're going to do anything without the Holy Spirit, don't do anything at all.

Did you understand that statement? If you're going to do something without the Holy Spirit, the easiest thing to do without Him is *nothing at all.* That's the best and the finest thing to do without Him. Do nothing and you won't get into trouble. Do nothing and you won't be a stumbling block to God's people and a detriment to God's work in the world. That's the one thing God in His grace and kindness allows us to do to please Him apart from His Holy Spirit. Nothing! (And really it doesn't please Him at all, because He wants us to use our gifts to bless and serve Christ's body, the church.)

The point is, do nothing…*until* you are filled with the Holy Spirit. And then—hang on to your hat, Jack! He'll have you doing things beyond what you ever imagined.

Are you willing to wait for God to move in your situation—whatever that situation may be? Every one of us has a situation where we have to wait on God. But none of us will get any spiritual brownie points for "just waiting," letting cobwebs grow in our eyebrows and weeds sprout up between our toes. God says not only do I want you to wait, but I want you to wait *in the right way* so you can graduate from My wait-control program. God, our fitness coach, wants to build us up spiritually, increasing our strength and endurance. If we spent half as much time trying to build our spiritual lives as we do our physical selves, we'd have some pretty buffed believers out there. (Check out 1 Timothy 4:8.)

Do nothing...until you are filled with the Holy Spirit.

Are you willing to wait for God's answers in your life...until *God* says it's long enough? I've talked to so many men and women who have run ahead of God in their impatience and fear and regretted it a million times over.

A FULL TANK

And when the day of Pentecost was fully come, they were all with one accord in one place. And suddenly there came a sound from heaven like a rushing mighty wind, and it filled all the house where they were sitting. And there appeared unto them cloven tongues as of fire, and it sat upon each of them. And they were all filled with the Holy Spirit, and began to speak with other tongues, as the Spirit gave them utterance (2:1–4).

What does it mean "when the day of Pentecost was fully come"? They had been celebrating Pentecost ever since the Passover. But *this* Pentecost was going to be like no other Pentecost. This

Pentecost would end an old era and usher in a new one.

The word "Pentecost" means fifty; in other words, fifty days after the Passover they celebrated Pentecost. This might give us a clue how long they waited and prayed in that upper room. All those long days and nights of waiting and then…the answer came roaring into their lives like a freight train!

I remember this past year visiting Jerusalem, and being startled by an odd wailing sound every morning at about five o'clock, and then again at about five o'clock in the evening. It was the call to prayer from the local mosque, and you could hear that thing all over the city.

Much of Israel itself is like an amplifier. The wind picks up your voice; it vibrates off all of those rocks, and you've got a good sounding board, Jack! So I can understand why it says the whole city came to investigate this Holy Spirit explosion.

When the Holy Spirit fills and controls you… people know there's something different about you.

It reminds me of the way it is before a tornado hits. It gets real quiet and then…the whole world seems to come unglued! I remember being in college at Livingston University when a tornado swept through town. Believe me, that thing put everyone on notice: "I'm here, and I'm mad! Just give me somethin' to tear up!"

The twister ripped through Livingston about twenty yards above the ground. Near the university a whole forest got topped out, just as if someone had come along with big shears and snapped the trees off as far as you could see. Instant buzz cut!

But what a sound! There's nothing like else like it. When you're close to a tornado it's like a thousand locomotives are charging by right over your roof—if you still have a roof!

Now…can you imagine all the sound pouring out of that one

house where the disciples were gathered? *Whooosh!* There goes the city's noise ordinance. Regardless of where you might have been in town that morning, you would dropped whatever you were doing. "What was THAT? Never heard anything like it before, let's go check it out!"

That's the way it is with the Holy Spirit. When God's Holy Spirit fills and controls you, all you have to do is walk into a room and people know there's something different about you. Frankly, some folks will be attracted by that "something different," and others will be repelled. That's okay! That's the way Scripture said it would be.

Paul wrote: "Thanks be to God who always leads us in triumph in Christ, and through us diffuses the fragrance of His knowledge in every place. For we are to God the fragrance of Christ among those who are being saved and among those who are perishing. To the one we are the aroma of death to death, and to the other the aroma of life to life" (2 Corinthians 2:14–16, NKJV).

In other words, the presence of Spirit-filled men and women will always make an impact. If that sort of thing isn't happening in your life, it could be because you're not allowing Him to fill you in that way. It's especially sad when you've been in the room for five years and still no one knows the difference!

> *The presence of Spirit-filled men and women will always make an impact.*

As the sound of a rushing wind poured out of that meeting place, the 120 men and women inside were instantly baptized and filled by the Holy Spirit. Don't confuse those two terms! They're totally different events. The baptism of the Spirit happens only once, when you and I become believers. In that moment, the Holy Spirit personally baptizes you into the body of Christ. In that same instant, He takes up permanent residence in your life. Your body becomes

His temple, and He will never leave you. In John 14:16–17, Jesus promised His men (and all of us): "I will pray the Father, and he shall give you another Comforter, that he may abide with you forever; even the Spirit of truth."

The filling or control of the Holy Spirit, on the other hand, is your submission to the Holy Spirit to lead you and guide you. Rather than a once-for-all event, this is something that has to happen every single day—and maybe even many times in a day.

I have to constantly submit myself to the Spirit and be filled with the Spirit, so that every time I wake up in the morning, or every time I start something new, or every time I approach an intersection in my life, I ask for His filling:

When I start a conversation on the sidewalk or in the hallway
When I pick up the phone
When I stare at this mug of mine through the steam on the
     shaving mirror
When I pick up a pen to write a note or memo
When I walk into the church building
When I step behind the pulpit
When I get into my truck
When I get stuck in traffic in my truck!

In those moments, in all of my moments, I need to be filled with the Holy Spirit. Why?

So that I might operate in His strength, not mine
So that I might speak His words
So that I might think His thoughts
So that I might see people and situations through His eyes
So that I might avoid the snares and traps of Satan

> So that I might be the hands and voice and presence of the
> Lord Jesus to someone who needs Him at any given
> moment

This is the very point where I believe the church today has lost so much of its power. We are not daily being filled and controlled by the mighty Spirit of God. We become weak and anemic in our faith because we can't even *feed* ourselves from God's Word apart from the filling of His Spirit. It is the Spirit's responsibility to reveal God, and if you're going to know God, you've got to know the Word! You need to be controlled by the supernatural presence of the Spirit to understand God's supernatural book, the Holy Bible.

That's why so many of us struggle as we try to get into the Word. We sit down for a minute or two and crack the cover of a Bible. But it's like swimming in jello; we can't make any headway. It seems so hard to understand—or just plain *boring*. Yet the truth is, there is nothing in this world as fresh and exciting as the Word of God when there are no unconfessed sins in your life and you're filled by the Spirit. God Himself becomes your tutor, showing you things about Himself, about the mysteries of His universe, about your own life, and about a million different situations as you read. Insights go off in your mind like a string of firecrackers exploding in a barrel.

It's dynamite!

That reminds me of a time, back in the old days, when you could kid around with security people at the airports. I was checking in at an airport one time, and had my Bible and a couple of other things in a bag. The security man said, "What do you have in that bag?"

I smiled at him and said, "Dynamite!" Then I showed him the Book.

You can't do that anymore! You'd be in jail for weeks! I can see it all now:

"Where's the pastor this morning?"

"Leavenworth."

"Leavenworth, Washington? That place up by Wenatchee?"

"No, the *other* Leavenworth. The one with bars on the windows and no souvenir shops."

The very first thing that happened to those believers at Pentecost, before the sign gift of speaking with other tongues, was the filling of God's Spirit. Guess what is the first thing that happens when you become a believer today? You are filled with the Holy Spirit. *Boom!* One hundred percent, nothing left out. He moves in and step by step, inch by inch, takes over the whole house. You may have accepted Him as Savior, but He moves in as Lord!

He doesn't come into your life to move into the attic. He wants the Master bedroom—and every other corner of the house, too. Count on it; when He moves into your life, He moves into *everything*. You may resist Him, you may quench Him, and you may grieve Him, but you can never evict Him! He's there to stay.

So what is the function of the Holy Spirit in our lives? The Holy Spirit is to fill, control, and empower believers. This is the secret of any and all success in the church. He fills believers to carry on the purpose of the church through all the years until His return.

WHAT'S GOING ON HERE?

Now when this was noised abroad, the multitude came together, and were confounded... (2:6).

I would guess so! God intended the church to be such a dynamic, powerful place that nonbelievers are drawn toward it in spite of themselves, because they want to know what in the world's going on with this bunch of people.

Following Peter's sermon in Acts 2, Scripture says that three thousand people were saved—and the church didn't even have an outreach program. What they had was a power outreach; and that's the way the church is supposed to be.

Filled with God's Spirit, we are to infiltrate those places where we work, where we live, where we go to school, so that people who see us and hear us and spend time with us can see the difference *When He moves* in our lives. And they say, "Man, I've got to go *into your life,* to church where he goes, or where she goes, *He moves into* and find out what's up!" So the first purpose *everything.* of the church is to make sure the members are full of the Holy Spirit and walking in Him.

When people outside of Christ see the *reality* of that kind of life, they'll be drawn to Him. With so much plastic phoniness in our world, the real thing always stands out. You can't miss it even if you *want* to miss it.

INTOXICATION!

And they were all amazed, and were perplexed, saying one to another, What meaneth this? Others, mocking, said, These men are full of new wine. But Peter, standing up with the eleven, lifted up his voice... (2:12–14).

Peter, my buddy!

About the only time he ever opened his mouth was to change feet. Peter! If he were alive today, he'd be a redneck living in Alabama with a rifle in the back window of his pickup. Peter, the man who boasted that *he* would never run or be afraid. No, not *him*. And then—at the most crucial moment—he didn't have enough guts to stand up to a little bitty girl.

"Oh, I know you, you're with Jesus."

"No, I'm not! Don't you say that—and if you weren't a girl I'd knock you out!"

He was too chicken to stand up to a little maid by the fireside, and now...here he is standing up in front of a huge crowd in the middle of Jerusalem, preaching the Word of God without fear. What's up? What made the difference?

I'll tell you the difference. Number one is confession. Number two is repentance. And number three is the filling of the Holy Spirit. As a result, Peter said, "I'll not only stand up and give you the message, but I'm going to say it *loud!*"

[Peter] lifted up his voice, and said unto them, Ye men of Judea, and all ye that dwell at Jerusalem, be this known unto you, and hearken to my words; For these are not drunk, as ye suppose... (2:14–15).

I love that! Some of the guys in the crowd had been laughing up their sleeves, saying, "These Galileans have been hitting the sauce. Look at 'em! They're drunker than skunks." But Peter comes back and says, "No, they're not drunk in the way that you're thinking." He never denied they were drunk! He just said it wasn't with *wine*. They were intoxicated with God's Holy Spirit!

Ephesians 5:18 says, "Be not drunk with wine...but be filled with the Spirit." Be filled with *the* Spirit, not with spirits. If you drink enough wine, the alcohol will make you say and do what you've been thinking about saying and doing but didn't have the guts to do. Under the control of alcohol, you'll do that and more! It will make you pull your car right alongside a police cruiser and say something stupid. It will make you walk up to a girl you've never seen before and say, "Hey girl, you good lookin' thing, let me take you out!" Make you look like an idiot.

Scripture says don't get drunk with that stuff; that's foolish excess. Get drunk with the Spirit of God. Be filled and controlled by Him.

Let's say you're fearful of talking to a certain person at work about the Lord. He or she seems hostile—and hard as a hunk of granite. Every time you start to speak to that person with a word of witness, it just dies in your throat. Let the Holy Spirit fill you, and, in His power, you'll say things you would have *never* said if you hadn't been "under the influence." Bible verses come out of your mouth you didn't even know that you knew!

You'll know you've been filled by the Holy Spirit when you look back over your day and say, "Oh my goodness, did I say that? Where did that come from?"

Peter says, "Drunk? They're not drunk with wine. What's up wit' chu? [That's the Hutcherson International Version.] It's only nine in the morning—get real! They haven't had enough time to get enough wine to be drunk!"

But they ARE full.

When people see someone who used to be a milquetoast now acting bold and fearless, they tend to say, "Ooh, what's wrong with him? What's up with her?" They know something's happened. They know that person is filled with something different than before. They know there's a new traffic controller up in that tower.

Many of us are afraid to speak up and tell the truth because we think it's going to turn people off to the gospel. Let me give you a little secret: You can't turn someone off who's never been *on*. They've only got one way to go. They can't get any more *off* than being bound for hell.

DON'T WAIT!

In Acts 4, Peter and John had been hauled before the Sanhedrin to explain why they continued to speak and heal in the name of Jesus. That was like being in front of Congress, the President, and the Supreme Court all rolled into one. It had to have been a scary moment. You might have expected Peter and John to lay low for a while; to do a little more listening than speaking.

But not Peter.

> And when they had set them in the midst, they asked, By what power, or by what name, have ye done this? Then Peter, filled with the Holy Spirit, said unto them, Ye rulers of the people, and elders of Israel… (4:7–8).

Boom! Peter doesn't look down at his sandals and mumble in his beard. He doesn't consult his lawyer or plead the Fifth Amendment. He's filled with the Spirit, and he can't wait to declare the Name again! The very Name those Jewish leaders dreaded to hear.

> Be it known unto you all, and to all the people of Israel, that by the name of Jesus Christ of Nazareth, whom ye crucified, whom God raised from the dead, even by him doth this man stand here before you whole (4:10).

I love it! "You guys have us on trial for speaking the name of Jesus? Well, I'm going to lay it on you again—and every chance I get!"

Tell me something, do you think Peter had to pause before he opened his mouth to seek the filling of the Spirit? I don't think so! I think Peter sought the filling of the Spirit from the time he opened his eyes in the jail cell that morning. I think he was so filled up that the Spirit came out right over the top and Peter couldn't contain Him. You see, when you get into a tough situation and suddenly ask the Spirit to fill you *then,* it may be a little late. But when that filling is an everyday, every moment proposition, you don't even break stride when you hit those tough times!

But even realizing you're *empty* can be a blessing. Here's what I mean:

- If you're sitting in a worship service and realize you've got problems with a brother or sister so that you just can't love them, you don't need to check out a book on love from the church library or go to a three-day seminar. *You need to fall on your knees and ask God to forgive you for not being controlled by His Spirit, so that you can love in His power.*

- If you're having a problem with self-discipline in your life so that you're causing problems and letting other people down, you don't need new organizer software for your computer. *You need to fall on your knees and ask God to forgive you and fill you with His Spirit. Then self-control is automatic through the Spirit of God.*

- If you find yourself paralyzed by fear in some area of your life so that your thoughts and emotions are locked up and you can't think of anyone but yourself, you don't need hypnosis or a therapist. *You need to fall on your knees and beg God to forgive you for not being controlled by His Spirit.*

- If you're always discontented with what you have and find yourself constantly daydreaming about more money, a bigger house, a better job, or a different wife or husband, you don't need to seek change in your situation. No, no, no! *You need to fall on your knees and ask God to forgive you for not allowing His Holy Spirit to overflow all of your empty places.*

If you know you're empty, that's good. Just remember to go to the right place to get filled! Don't go to the bar. Don't go to the drug dealer. Don't run to pornography or fantasies. Don't try to fill the hole with money or success or busyness. Let the Lord fill you up with the Holy Spirit and you'll have all the power and joy you've been looking for—and more besides.

Let's talk to Him about it right now.

Lord, thank You for Your Word.

You know I don't know Greek or Hebrew. Sometimes I think I barely know English. But I do know You! And I have Your Holy Spirit to fill all of my empty places. And Father, because of Your gift of the Holy Spirit, I don't have an excuse for leading a substandard life.

Your Spirit eliminates the statement "I can't do it."

Your Spirit eliminates the excuse "I just can't forgive."

Your Spirit eliminates the complaint "I just can't understand this Bible."

Your mighty Holy Spirit living inside of us eliminates any and everything that keep us from being molded into the image of Your Son. Because that's His job, and nobody does it better than He does. The Holy Spirit says He's come to give us power and to give the church power. And may we all come to the realization, Lord, that if there are problems, I'm looking right in the face of the main problem every day when I look in the mirror. The only hindrance to Your allowing me to be what I need to be and You want me to be is *me*. It isn't anyone else. There is no excuse for not living a righteous life.

So Lord, I pray now that if there are believers reading these words who have habits, hang-ups, or motives that they know are not pure, may they this day, this moment, ask You to forgive them. Wipe them clean. Control them by Your Spirit, that they may walk into a new day with power—*dynamo* power that builds and builds—and a changed life to match.

And Lord, we know that as we believers walk with You controlled by Your Spirit, the world does not have a chance. None. Evangelism is automatic because everyone wants the truth.

In Jesus' most holy, precious, and glorious name, we all say amen.

Because We Aren't in the Word

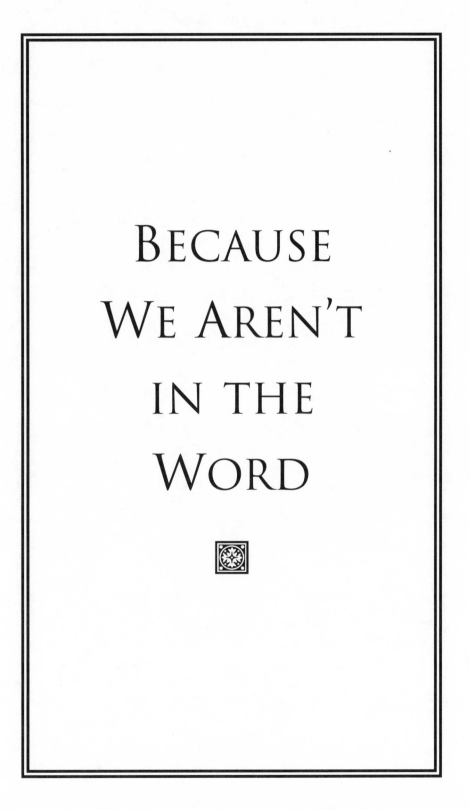

CHAPTER 2

W e've made things very, very complicated in the church today.

If you don't think so, it's probably because you've been on the inside looking out so long, you've forgotten what it all looks like to people on the outside looking in. Those outside of church circles, if they're even interested at all, can feel bewildered by what they see. Denominations...theological labels...conferences...traditions...conventions...worship styles. It gets confusing.

We've got High Church and Low Church. We've got fundamentalists, evangelicals, neoevangelicals, and mainliners. We've got charismatic and noncharismatic, traditional and contemporary. We've got Free Methodists and United Methodists. We've got multiple-choice Presbyterians, a rainbow variety of Lutherans, and more flavors of Baptists than Heinz has pickles.

But for all our denominational options, the church isn't doing well in our contemporary culture. And the reason it isn't doing well is because we've lost our simple emphasis on teaching the Word of God.

The Bible is all about life change.

The Bible is all about life change. It's about drawing people into the power and wisdom of the Holy Spirit. It's about filling a man or woman's veins with the very life of Jesus Christ. In the church at Antioch, the believers' lives were so changed and so radically different from those around them that folks in town started calling them "little Christs," or *Christians*.

Most people have forgotten where the word "Christian" came from, or what it means. As far as our contemporary world is concerned, it doesn't mean much of anything. And there's a reason for that: the church today has been caught up in just about everything except what God intended us to be caught up in—the saving, restoring, convicting, eternal Word of almighty God.

FOOLISH PREACHING?

The apostle Paul wrote something a little bit strange to the church in Corinth:

> Where is the wise? Where is the scribe? Where is the disputer of this age? Hath not God made foolish the wisdom of this world? For after that, in the wisdom of God, the world by wisdom knew not God, it pleased God by the foolishness of preaching to save them that believe (1 Corinthians 1:20–21).

Isn't that amazing? God says He chose the *foolishness* of preaching to save the world! Ooh, I don't know if I like that! Preaching is what I do for a living. Preaching is my life. And God calls it foolishness? That's what He said. And yet, foolish or not, it's the means He has chosen to save the world. Preachers *can* be foolish...some more than others. The only thing that's not foolish about preaching is the Word of God itself.

Get filled up, fueled up, prayed up, fired up... and then give witness.

If the church today wants to line up with the desire and heart of God, we had better make sure that there is more time spent teaching and preaching the Word of God than *any* other activity. It has to be priority number one. Strip away everything else—all the stained glass, the padded pews, the music, the programs, the activities, the bulletins, the announcements—and the church will still survive. (Did I say thrive? I did not say thrive!) But it cannot survive without the preaching of the Word of God.

What, then, should we be preaching? Evangelism?

That's what takes place all week as the church scatters. But the church gathers on the Lord's day for the teaching and preaching of the Word, the whole Word, the whole counsel of God. It drives me absolutely nuts when people come to church expecting to hear a salvation message every Sunday. Sunday is when God's people need to be *taught*. Our responsibility is to get filled up, fueled up, prayed up, fired up, and then go out in the world and give witness to what we've learned.

Monday through Saturday, we're supposed to get out of our comfort zones.

Ninety percent of the Bible, after all, is addressed to believers, telling us how we should live, how we should talk, and how we should conduct ourselves. Only 10 percent deals with salvation. So why should I, as a preacher, spend 90 percent of my time teaching just 10 percent of the Bible?

Monday through Saturday, we're supposed to disperse, get out of our comfort zones, and tell the world, "Man, Sunday I got *filled*—now sit down and listen to this! I've got to give it to somebody or I'm going to burst!"

The Holy Spirit came at Pentecost to fill *believers*. And that same Holy Spirit is the author of the Bible. The principal purpose of the Word, then, is to edify, or build up believers. When you are filled by the Spirit so that you understand and apply His Word to your life, when the Spirit shines the light of understanding in your mind and in your spirit, when the Spirit emboldens you to speak to the unbelievers who cross your path on any given day, you'll have something to say!

The Bible is written to believers to get off their duffs to go out and win the nonbelieving world. And to do that, believers must be equipped.

That's my job. I like my job. It's the big desire of my heart to see God's people both *equipped* and *prepared* to be God's ambassadors in a hostile world.

Thinking about equipment reminds me of growing up in the South, when we couldn't afford much sports equipment. As boys who loved to play ball, we just had to make do with what we had. For a football, we'd take a rock and cover it with a bunch of socks (the more the better). It worked pretty good for passing, but you didn't want to take your eyes off the ball when you were running out for a pass because if that thing hit you on the head it might kill you.

When we were shooting baskets, we'd use an old tire rim for a basketball goal.

On our Little League baseball team, however, we had a coach who wanted us to really look good. Mr. Broom was very concerned about appearances. So instead of spending our time practicing (like we should have been doing), we were out selling candy bars door to door—raising money for uniforms!

One little kid was an especially good salesman. He probably sold enough candy to buy three uniforms because he was so excited to be on a baseball team. As a matter of fact, he was often out hawking candy bars when the rest of us were practicing. On the day of our first game, we were all out on the field in that new gear, and man, we were lookin' *good*. We were trying to decide who was going to start—and of course we had to let our little salesman take the field. After all, he'd made a major contribution to those uniforms.

But the sad truth was, if the first-teamers hadn't got much practice, this little guy had hardly had any (we're talking about maybe .5 hours). The other team was at bat, and we let our little salesman take his place in center field. Almost right away, one of the batters connected—a high pop fly headed for…guess where?

Our little fielder went into motion. He yelled, "I got it! I got it! I got it!" Trouble was, he stuck his glove in the air too soon. He had that glove up above his head, waiting for the ball to come down. But the wait was too long for him. And where was that ball? He couldn't see past his glove. So he pulled it down for a second to check out the situation just as the ball completed its arch and—*crack*—smacked him right on top of the head.

"Without the Word I have no words."

He screamed and grabbed his head, then took off running for home.

"Hey!" we yelled. "Where you goin'?"

He yelled back, "I quit! I QUIT!"

Lack of preparation had killed that boy's enthusiasm—and our whole team's chances to win any games that year. But boy, did we look good!

As a preacher and teacher of the Word, it's my task to see that believers are both equipped *and* prepared. So this old black football player is going to spend the majority of his time preaching to believers. Because if believers get fired up with the Word and under control of the Holy Spirit, the nonbelieving world doesn't have a chance.

"HEY, LISTEN UP!"

"Ye men of Judea, and all ye that dwell at Jerusalem, be this known unto you, and hearken to my words; for these are not drunk, as ye suppose, seeing it is but the third hour of the day. But this is that which was spoken through the prophet, Joel…" (Acts 2:14–16).

In Peter's first sermon to the Jews after the church was born, he

The miracle got their attention, but the main event was the teaching of God's Word.

stood up, lifted his voice, and said, "Hearken to my words." Or, in other words, "Hey, listen up!" And then what does he do? He takes them right into their own Scriptures.

He says "listen to my words" and then he takes them into THE Word. To put it another way, "My word is the Word. Without the Word I have no words." So at the beginning of God's new work in the world—at the very dawn of the church age—a Spirit-filled man raises his voice, opens the Book, and begins to teach the Scriptures.

> "And it shall come to pass in the last days, saith God, I will pour out of my Spirit upon all flesh; and your sons and your daughters shall prophesy, and your young men shall see visions, and your old men shall dream dreams; and on my servants and on my handmaidens I will pour out in those days of my Spirit, and they shall prophesy" (2:17–18).

Do you see what's happened here?

The Holy Spirit starts things rolling with a miraculous sign gift—the miracle of speaking with other tongues, which drew all of those people together in sheer amazement and wonder—and then God's servant moved right into the teaching of God's Word.

The sign gift gathered a crowd, the miracle got their attention, but the main event was the teaching of God's Word.

Do you want to grow? Get in the Word.

Do you want to have power? Be filled with the Word.

Do you want to have victory? Be controlled by the Spirit so He can teach you the Word.

Do you want to make a difference in the lives of those who are watching your life? Live the Word.

After all the smoke and fire have cleared away, it is the Word of God that gets God's business done.

Signs and wonders and miracles have their place in God's scheme of things, and I have seen miracles in my own life that would make your curly hair straight (or your straight hair curly, as the case may be). But after all the smoke and fire have cleared away, it is the Word that gets God's business done.

THE WORD: IT'S ALL ABOUT JESUS

"Whom God hath raised up, having loosed the pains of death, because it was not possible that he should be held by it" (2:24).

Peter confronted them with the truth of the resurrected Christ, and they were "pricked in their heart" (2:37). You cannot run from the truth about Christ! You can run to another religion, another persuasion, another philosophy. You can even run to atheism. But you can't get away from the Truth. Sooner or later, on this side of eternity or on the other side, you'll have to face it.

Then why, you might ask me again, don't we preach the gospel of Jesus Christ all the time? Why don't we come back to it Sunday after Sunday? The truth is, every time I open my Bible, from Genesis to Revelation, I'm preaching Jesus Christ. It's *all* about Him. It's all His story. Because beyond the printed Word of God, He is the living Word of God. "In the beginning was the

Word, and the Word was with God, and the Word was God" (John 1:1).

So anytime I open the Book I'm going to say what the Word, Jesus Christ, is saying. The whole Bible is centered around Jesus. You don't have to give a "gospel message" every Sunday, but you do have to give the Word. And as you do, Jesus is going to be glorified and the church is going to get organized around the truth.

When the risen Jesus was walking with the two men on the road to Emmaus, He began talking to them about the resurrection, and then put it ALL in context for them by declaring the Word.

> And beginning at Moses and all the prophets, he expounded unto them, in all the scriptures, the things concerning himself (Luke 24:27).

Again, just before He was taken up to heaven, Jesus said to His disciples,

> "These are the words which I spoke unto you, while I was yet with you, that all things must be fulfilled, which were written in the law of Moses, and in the prophets, and in the psalms, concerning me." Then opened he their understanding, that they might understand the scriptures (Luke 24:44–45).

As my man Scofield writes, "Cleopas and his companion on the Emmaus Road had the inestimable privilege of hearing the incarnate Word, Christ the risen Lord, expound the written Word, the Holy Scriptures. In doing so, the Lord Jesus gave them the great key to the understanding of Scripture—that He Himself is its subject and that in Him the entire Book finds its unity."

"MORE, MORE! WE WANT MORE!"

Then they that gladly received his word were baptized; and the same day there were added unto them about three thousand souls. And they continued steadfastly in the apostles' doctrine and fellowship, and in breaking of bread, and in prayers (2:41–42).

Whoa! Blow down the doors!

That day, church growth was out of control. And what did it look like? They fellowshiped and continued steadfastly in the disciples' doctrine. In other words, they *devoured* the Word of God. *More, more, we want more! Give us more! We can't get enough!*

Man, if we could get today's church excited that way! It's hard to get most believers excited about five minutes of Bible study a day. There's even a product on the Christian market today called the *One-Minute Bible.* As if sixty seconds in the Word can equip us for everything we'll face in a given day. What if that was all the time you had to eat food for the whole day? I could

Good digestion requires some chewing. Good understanding of Scripture requires time and thought.

probably eat quite a bit in one minute if I had to, but then the rest of the day I'd have indigestion.

Good digestion requires some chewing. Good understanding of Scripture requires some time and thought.

These people were steadfast. In other words, they were *continually* in the Word. They kept after it.

No wonder there was so much power shining out of that place! No wonder these believers were accused of turning the world upside down.

OBEDIENCE BEFORE PROGRAMS!

Then they that gladly received his word were baptized; and the same day there were added unto them about three thousand souls (2:41).

Three thousand people joined the church at one time. *Boom!*

What would happen at most churches if that happened today? Can't you just hear the church leaders wringing their hands and moaning, "Oh, OH! What are we going to do? There aren't enough Sunday school rooms! There aren't enough communion cups! There aren't enough pews! And the nursery, oh my land, the *nursery!* What are we going to do with all the babies! Where are we going to get enough Pampers? Who's going to bake all those cookies for fellowship time? We haven't got our training programs up and running! We haven't finished adding the graphics to our manuals! What are we going to *do* with these three thousand people?"

Let me tell you a secret. We can get so caught up in programs and procedures and what we don't have and ought to have and used to have that we get paralyzed. God wouldn't dare send us three thousand people, because it would upset all our plans. It would ruin our day. We wouldn't know what to do with all those new Christians.

Peter's game plan was pretty simple. He taught the Word.

He just laid it out there and let God worry about church growth. He knew that if God brought the increase, He was big enough and strong enough and wise enough and had enough resources to take care of that increase. Like Peter, we need to be caught up in the Word of God. But instead we're caught up in all of our programs and seminars. And we wonder why there's no power!

Three thousand souls! That kind of works a hardship on those folks who like nice, quiet little churches, doesn't it? The fact is, God dictates the growth. Not me, not you.

If you are living the Word of God you're going to be obedient to the Word of God. If you are obedient to the Word of God, you're going to evangelize, you're going to disciple, you're going to be concerned about needs in the body, you're going to have compassion for the poor, you're going to learn more about the Word and make your life line up with the Word so that you look more and more like Jesus Himself. Then, after you've saturated yourself in the Scriptures and you're walking in fullhearted obedience, you can add the "program."

Let me say it another way. You and I don't make programs in the church; we're called to be obedient to the Word, and that *obedience* gives birth to a program. We've got too many people trying to make a program without first being obedient, without first learning from the Word what the heart of God really cares about. That's why so many programs (and churches) fail.

Does that get you excited? Thinking about this just gives me faith bumps! You see, this is what the church is all about: to bring you in line with the Word of God, so that everything that is taught is going to be done. When people understand the Scriptures and the daily filling of the Spirit, they begin to exercise their gifts in obedience to the Word of God. And when you've got enough people being obedient in any given area, *then* you've got a program. And guess what? It really works!

You and I tend to take these things for granted because we've been in the church for a long time. But here in the book of Acts, it was all fresh. The paint was still wet. The church of Jesus Christ was something brand new in the world. They didn't have any traditions or denominations or seminaries or instruction manuals in three-ring binders to tell them how to do it. That's why the apostles had to write all the letters and say, This is the way we are supposed to behave and practice; this is the Word of God.

I'd like to ask you a simple question: What if the Word was all we had?

Is that a revolutionary thought? It's a little scary, isn't it?

What if we were starting fresh, with only the Word of God to guide us and the Spirit of God to open our understanding? How much extra baggage would get thrown out the window? How many books and manuals would get sent to the shredder? What would the church look like if all we had was a passion to obey the Word of God? How would we be organized?

Do you think the Spirit of God is able to reinvent the church as we step into a new century and a new millennium?

PETER'S FIRST PRINCIPLES

Try to imagine those three thousand people, all coming into the church on one fine, sunny morning. What were Peter's first instructions?

> Then Peter said unto them, Repent, and be baptized, every one of you, in the name of Jesus Christ for the remission of sins, and ye shall receive the gift of the Holy Spirit. For the promise is unto you, and to your children, and to all that are afar off, even as many as the Lord, our God, shall call (2:38–39).

Repent.

What is "repent"? It means to change your mind, to turn away from the way you used to do things. And by the way, God is not interested in 90-degree turns. He's holding out for 180 degrees. But some of us neglect the Word of God and so we either content ourselves with half turns or go too far and spin ourselves around 270 degrees! But God's not interested in imbalance, He's interested in real life change.

To get it down to where we live, to repent means the things I used to do I can't do anymore. The things that used to occupy my thoughts and occupy all my time (especially if those things run contrary to the Word of God) have changed. I have a new life. I have a new lifestyle.

> And with many other words did he testify and exhort, saying, Save yourselves from this crooked generation (2:40).

When you repent, guess who else you are repenting from? Your old friends. Your old associations. Your old haunts. You see, a lot of us want to change as Christians, but we don't want to give up our old buddies.

As a baby believer you're probably not strong enough to influence your old friends. You haven't fed on the Word long enough. You haven't walked in the Spirit long enough. They're probably stronger in their own ways than you are as a Christian, so you may have to pull away from them for a while.

That doesn't mean that you should write them off! They need the Lord, too. They need someone to care about them and talk to them about salvation in Christ. Yet Scripture says clearly that we need to draw away from this corrupt generation and all it stands for. Peter describes the generation that crucified the Lord Jesus as crooked or perverse. And let's not kid ourselves; the generation we're living in now isn't any different. If anything, it's worse. If the Lord Jesus were here again, our world would try to crucify Him all over again. And it probably wouldn't take us three and a half years!

So it doesn't really matter how "nice" or "fun" those old non-Christian friends are. They're going to pull you in the wrong direction, regardless of how nice they may be. So you need to remove yourself from that influence for a time, until you've grown stronger in the Lord.

"Repent, and be baptized, every one of you, in the name of Jesus Christ..." (2:38).

Right. So they repented and...now the apostles have to baptize three thousand people!

There are old James and John and Peter and Thomas, dunkin' them as fast as they can. "Two hundred eighty-five, two hundred eighty-six, two hundred eighty-seven...hey, Nathanael, can you give me a hand over here? My back's killin' me, bro! That last Pharisee must have weighed three hundred pounds!"

They devoured the apostles' words... like hungry teenagers with their faces in the refrigerator.

We don't think about that kind of stuff! But baptizing three thousand people was a pretty tall order, and it took some serious obedience. Now that I think about it, maybe that's how some of the other traditions got started. After about a thousand immersions, those exhausted apostles might have said, "Hoo boy, that's enough! Let's just sprinkle 'em and call it a day!"

BEYOND COOKIES AND BAD PUNCH

And they continued steadfastly in the apostles' doctrine and fellowship... (2:42).

Those baby believers just *devoured* the apostles' words. They were like hungry teenagers with their faces in the refrigerator. They were like three thousand sponges trying to soak up every word that spilled out of the apostles' mouths.

But what do we try to do with new believers? We try to give them all kinds of information about "how to get busy." But the truth is, if you're head over heels in love with God's Word, being obedient to the Word, you'll *be* busy doing the right things, not just doing "busy work."

As they were devouring the Word, they had fellowship with each other. And it was the right kind of fellowship. The Greek word is *koinonia*.

You see, most people think "fellowship" is Kool-Aid and cookies after the service. But true *koinonia* doesn't mean beverage service and a sugar high. It means a relationship of holding one another accountable to what you're learning from the Word of God. I make sure you're living the Word, and you're checking me out to make sure I'm living the Word. *That's* fellowship. And you can throw some sistership in there, too!

Besides all that, church punch is the worst thing in the world. It's an abomination. I think it's become some kind of doctrine through the years that church punch just *has* to taste bad. But sipping bad cherry punch and eating stale, store-bought cookies isn't fellowship, it's just spending a little time together so we can go on our merry way. No, fellowship occurs when you and I are in the Scriptures together and holding each other accountable to the standards of the Word.

WARMIN' UP FOR THE MAIN EVENT

And fear came upon every soul; and many wonders and signs were done by the apostles (2:43).

Acts 2:43 is something like an umbrella, a verse that spreads out and covers a lot of ground. The upshot is that God was doing signs and wonders through the apostles to draw people's attention and underline His Word during this transitional period. In Acts 2, it was the miracle of believers speaking with languages they'd never learned, declaring "the wonderful works of God" (2:11).

And in Acts 3, the Holy Spirit is going to move in yet a different way to gather a great crowd for Peter's second sermon: the amazing healing of a man who had been lame from birth.

Both sign gifts served the purpose of gathering a crowd. And when the people were assembled, Peter preached the Word of God. The miracles and wonders were just the preliminaries to the preaching of the Word. Have you ever been to a concert to hear a certain group or band, and before your heroes take the stage, they bring out another group just to warm things up? As soon as the first band begins to play, people say, "Ooh, something's happenin.' I'd better find my seat." That's how I think of these miracles. They got people in the door, they got the crowd moving, but they weren't the main act. The main thing is always the teaching of God's Word.

God used the great miracles to bring out the crowds and to draw His church together. That's why you don't see the sign gift used as much anymore, because we have an established pattern in the church. Now, what did I say? Did I say I don't *believe* in sign gifts? No, no, no. If you tell someone I said that, we're going to have to have a little talk. And I'm probably bigger than you!

We have preliminaries in today's church, too. Good preliminaries. There's nothing wrong with them. But if those preliminaries are serving their true purpose, they're getting us ready to hear and respond to God's Word. We can sometimes find ourselves disagreeing and disputing about those preliminaries. You can't believe how bitter it becomes! One likes this style of music, another likes a different style of music, and still others don't like music at all. Some like the announcements and offering before the message, some insist that they ought to be after the message, and others think they ought to be done away with altogether. The point, however, is that these are preliminaries. The substance is the preaching and teaching of the Word. If we're caught up in arguing over preliminaries, we've lost the whole point of our gathering.

THE PURPOSE OF MIRACLES

Now Peter and John went up together into the temple at the hour of prayer, being the ninth hour. And a certain man lame from his mother's womb was carried, whom they laid daily at the gate of the temple which is called Beautiful, to ask alms of them that entered into the temple; who seeing Peter and John about to go into the temple asked an alms. And Peter, fastening his eyes upon him with John, said, Look on us. And he gave heed unto them, expecting to receive something of them. Then Peter said, Silver and gold have I none; but such as I have give I thee: In the name of Jesus Christ of Nazareth rise up and walk. And he took him by the right hand, and lifted him up: and immediately his feet and ankle bones received strength. And he leaping up stood, and walked, and entered with them into the temple, walking, and leaping, and praising God (3:1–8).

The fact is, miracles were not given to produce contentment or faith. That's not the purpose of miracles. Miracles are a sign to everybody that God is doing something in the midst of His people.

Now you better get involved to find out what that something is! We have come to the conclusion that the preaching of the Word of God is the center, the most important aspect of worship. Everything else is to lead you to the Word of God, to draw you right into the Truth. As the apostles preached about Jesus—crucified, risen from the dead, and coming again—that's what got people saved.

It wasn't the gift of tongues that saved people. It wasn't any miraculous healing that saved people. Those events were like rocket flares sent up into the sky. Fireworks! Oohs and aahs. After they gathered a crowd and got people's attention, it was the preaching of the Word that knifed into hard hearts and brought thousands into the infant church.

The miracles themselves didn't produce belief. It seems like they *should* have, but they didn't. If they had, the leaders of the Jews would have been the first to bow the knee to Christ. These leaders had seen, heard, and thoroughly discussed the miracles of the Lord Jesus…and they ended up nailing Him to a cross!

If miracles were going to lead to salvation and faith, who should have been the first ones to walk down the sawdust aisle after this man born lame was healed at the Beautiful Gate?

The whole Sanhedrin!

Why? Because they had the man standing right in front of them with the ones who healed him in the name of Jesus Christ. They knew very well something supernatural had occurred. But there was no indication (in spite of what they admitted was a "notable miracle") that any of their rock-hard hearts budged even a single inch.

Why? Because that wasn't the purpose of the miracles.

What is the purpose for gifts? What is the purpose for signs? What is the purpose for wonders? *It is to draw attention to the teaching of the Word.*

So often in churches today we hear the teaching that certain gifts of the Spirit will make you stronger, move you closer to God, or elevate you to some new level of spirituality. But Scripture never teaches that gifts were given to draw you closer to God or elevate you to a new plateau of saintliness. And that's why we're so disappointed when we try to use them in that fashion. They simply weren't given for that purpose.

The purpose of the gifts and miracles was to draw attention to a new thing God was doing in the world: changing hearts and lives through the salvation of Jesus Christ and the indwelling of the Holy Spirit. And as the culture of that day saw lives being changed and people using their gifts, they said, "Whoa, this is something different! Something new! Maybe it's of God. Let's go check it out." And then they too heard the preaching of the Word and learned the truth about their sin and the truth about Christ's offer of salvation.

That's about the time folks were ripping the doors down, so many wanted into the kingdom. Bottom line: It isn't miracles or gifts or supernatural fireworks that save men and women from hell, it is the word of truth.

CAUGHT UP IN THE WORD

Today in the church we get caught up in this gift and that gift, this ability and that ability, this color and that color, this style of music and that style of music. We get caught up in everything except what the church should be centered around, and that is: what does the Bible have to say about Jesus?

We see people leave a particular church and drag the family all over town, not because of what that church teaches about Christ, but because of some minor tradition or practice. We have people leave a church because of what that church says (or doesn't say) about a particular gift of the Spirit. We have people leave a church because of what the leadership says (or doesn't say) about community involvement or certain political issues.

You show me anywhere in Scripture that says we ought to be caught up in those things! If we're obedient to the Word of God in Jesus Christ, all the peripheral matters will fall into place. We'll find ourselves caught up in that which catches up the heart of God.

THE ONLY BASIS FOR UNITY

What do individual churches give up to unite with denominations or ecumenical movements? What truths do they surrender? What errors do they have to swallow? What is the price of "fellowship" that compromises the Word of God?

Paul didn't pussyfoot around with the church in Galatia. He reminds me a little of a linebacker; he took the direct approach. "Though we, or an angel from heaven, preach any other gospel unto you than that which we have preached unto you, let him be accursed" (Galatians 1:8).

Oh my goodness, this man is being radical! He couldn't have meant that. But he did mean it. And just in case they might have (somehow) missed the point, he said it again in the very next verse. *Boom, boom!*

Did you know that was in the Bible? But here we are today trying our best to "just get along." I call this Rodney King theology. (You remember him: "Why can't we all just get along?") But this isn't the church of Rodney King, it is the church of Jesus Christ. And if we're going to be unified, we must be unified according to the changeless, timeless, inerrant, eternal Word of God.

Everything else has to take a back seat.

IT'S ALL IN THE BOOK

Now there were in the church that was at Antioch certain prophets and teachers, as Barnabas, and Symeon, who was called Niger, and Lucius of Cyrene, and Manaen, who had been brought up with Herod, the tetrarch, and Saul (Acts 13:1).

Symeon, who was called *what?*
Niger? You won't mispronounce that word in my neighbor-

hood! It better not rhyme with Roy Roger's horse, or you could find yourself in trouble.

> As they ministered to the Lord, and fasted, the Holy Spirit said, Separate me Barnabas and Saul for the work unto which I have called them. And when they had fasted and prayed, and laid their hands on them, they sent them away (13:2–3).

Symeon (more about this black church leader later!), Barnabas, Saul, and others are called "prophets and teachers" here. The author, Dr. Luke, uses the familiar word "prophet." But the term was already changing in this transitional book between the Old and New Testaments. Later in the book, Paul drops the word "prophet" and begins talking about "pastors and teachers."

A prophet today is totally different than a prophet in the days of Isaiah or Jeremiah. He is to declare what God has *already* spoken. A modern-day prophet is just a pastor or teacher who stands up and says, "Thus saith the Lord," and then opens the pages of Scripture. All that God wants to say to men and women is already there in the Book; there is no need of new revelation. If someone says to you, "God told me something new," just shrug your shoulders and walk away. You don't need to hear about it because they don't have anything new. God has said what He wants to say, and it's all between the two covers of the Holy Bible. In the Old Testament sense of the term, the church today is a nonprophet organization!

"Can't God say anything new?" you ask me. Well, I'll tell you what…when I learn how to live according to the sixty-six books I've already got, maybe God will give me another one. Until then, until I've learned to be wholehearted and obedient toward what

I've already received (give me a millennium or two), don't talk to me about some new revelation. I've got all I can handle with the revelation I've got!

That would be just like one of your kids coming up to you and asking you for $100 when you just gave them $1,000 that they badly misused. What kind of parent is going to shell out another hundred bucks—except an irresponsible parent who just wants the kids out of his hair?

God has provided us with the complete Instruction Manual for living life on planet Earth. As Paul put it:

> All scripture is given by inspiration of God, and is profitable for doctrine, for reproof, for correction, for instruction in righteousness, that the man of God may be perfect, thoroughly furnished unto all good works (2 Timothy 3:16–17).

Read the Instruction Manual! When you learn it all and live it all (and you never will), *then* you'll be ready for something new.

But don't hold your breath.

BECAUSE WE EXPECT CHURCH TO BE "COMFORTABLE"

CHAPTER 3

Now when this was noised abroad, the multitude came together, and were confounded, because every man heard them speak in his own language. And they were all amazed and marveled, saying one to another...How hear we every man in our own tongue, wherein we were born? (Acts 2:6–7, 8)

Acts tells the story of a world opened up for the church of Jesus Christ. It tells the story of how a church, a society of "called-out ones," was founded by Christ for all peoples, nations, and cultures.

Pentecost is a small picture of what the church would become. At Pentecost, people from all surrounding nations heard believers "speak in our tongues the wonderful works of God" (2:11).

By the way, they not only heard the gospel in their own languages, they heard it in their own *dialects*. To a woman from the Bronx in New York City, it would have sounded just like home. And the same for the coal miner in Appalachia, the surfer dude in Southern California, and the guy who runs the Waffle Shop in Birmingham, Alabama.

At the tower of Babel, the races and languages scattered in different directions all over the globe. But at Pentecost, after the

Lamb of God was sacrificed for the sins of the whole world, for the first time God allowed all people of all nations to hear the gospel in their own language and dialect, calling them back from isolation and separation.

Pentecost declared, "The church is for all races and all people. Anywhere the church of Jesus Christ meets, a member of God's family ought to be able to walk in and feel at home."

As believers, we have "put on the new man who is renewed in knowledge according to the image of Him who created him, where there is neither Greek nor Jew, circumcised nor uncircumcised, barbarian, Scythian, slave nor free, but Christ is all and in all" (Colossians 3:10–11, NKJV).

Sunday morning worship is the most segregated hour in America.

The church was to declare to the nations, "God is alive, Jesus is Savior and Lord, and everybody has a place in God's family." But we haven't followed God's pattern and plan, have we? In most places in our country today, we're still trying to live the Old Testament by keeping races and nationalities separate on Sunday morning. It's sad, but true: Sunday morning worship is still the most segregated hour in America.

Different races and cultures in our country rub shoulders all week long in school, in the workplace, in movie theaters, in shopping malls, and at sporting events. But on Sundays? We all scatter for our little homogeneous groupings to worship the Lord.

I think that must grieve the heart of Christ, who gave His very life to create one new, unified body...His church.

For He Himself is our peace, who has made both one, and has broken down the middle wall of division between us, having abolished in His flesh the enmity...so as to create in Himself one new man from the two, thus making peace, and that He might reconcile them both to God in one body through the cross, thereby putting to death the enmity (Ephesians 2:14–16, NKJV).

That's what the Book says. But that's not what the church looks like today.

PHILIP TAKES THE LEAD

Then Philip went down to the city of Samaria, and preached Christ unto them (Acts 8:5).

Do you understand how powerful this verse is?

Just imagine it's 1962, and the text reads, "Then Philip pole-vaulted over the Berlin Wall to East Berlin and preached Christ to the Communist border guards."

Or imagine it reading, "Then Philip walked into a Catholic neighborhood in Belfast, Northern Ireland, and began holding a Protestant street meeting."

Or imagine if it read, "Then Ken Hutcherson walked into a Ku Klux Klan meeting in Mississippi, smiled and said, 'Yo, Wiz,' to the Imperial Wizard, and began walking up and down the aisles handing out gospel tracts."

That would take a little nerve! What Philip did was every bit as amazing. The church in Jerusalem had been scattered by a wave of persecution, but as Philip hightailed it out of town, he had the right idea: "Hey, as long as I'm on the road, I may as well spread the Word of God every chance I get. Ooh, what's that place up ahead? Looks like Samaria. What should I do? Well, when in doubt, I may as well preach Christ. I can't go far wrong with that method!"

The Samaritans and the Jews *hated* each other. When Jesus Christ gave the command to take the gospel to Jerusalem, Judea, and Samaria in Acts 1:8, there must have been those within earshot who thought He was kidding. *"Samaria? That's got to be a slip of the tongue. Maybe He meant to say 'some area,' and it just sounded like Samaria!"*

The Jews called the Samaritans half-breeds—and that's when they were being polite. It was a feud that dated back hundreds of years to the time when the conquering Assyrians brought people in from the surrounding regions and settled them in northern Israel. These folks, inter-marrying with the Jews left behind in conquered territory, adopted some of the Jewish customs and Scriptures, but not all of them. To the "pure-bred" Jews, even talking to one of these people was unthinkable.

All Philip did was to chuck hundreds of years of prejudice and racial hatred into the Dumpster.

When Jesus stopped to chat with the Samaritan prostitute at the well in the village of Sychar, the woman was so startled she forgot all about her water jar and sprinted back into town to get a party together (see John 4).

The Jews hated the Samaritans so much that whenever they were traveling from Judea to Galilee, they would stop at the border of Samaria, cut across the Jordan, go up on the opposite side of the Jordan, then recross the Jordan to come into Galilee. It was a long way around, especially when you were walking. But there was so much enmity there they wouldn't even put their foot down on the other guy's turf.

All Philip did was to chuck hundreds of years of prejudice and racial hatred into the Dumpster on his way out of Jerusalem. He said to himself, "Well, Jesus said 'Samaria,' so why not *me* and why not *now?*"

This was not Philip the apostle, because the text has already said that the apostles remained behind in Jerusalem. This was Philip the deacon, the man who was chosen along with Stephen and other Spirit-filled men as special servants to the church.

Philip went on this mission not because it was such a great job, but because the intense persecution had finally squeezed him out of Jerusalem. As a matter of fact, it had been so tense and dangerous back home in Jerusalem that ol' Samaria looked pretty good when he walked into town. The fact is, God knows how to make us uncomfortable where we are so that the uncomfortable situation we're walking into doesn't feel all that uncomfortable.

Don't tell me you can't get over old prejudices!

That's one positive result of persecution!

> And they, when they had testified and preached the word of the Lord, returned to Jerusalem, and preached the gospel in many villages of the Samaritans (8:25).

Isn't that something? As Philip and some of the others who had joined him were going back to Jerusalem, they took time to preach Jesus in village after village across Samaria. It's like they were having so much fun they really didn't want to go home.

"Hey, there's another village. All right! More Samaritans! Let's stay another night!" They'd already forgotten centuries of hatred and prejudice and old negative baggage. They'd thrown aside all those separatist messages that had been drilled into their heads since they were in diapers. Don't tell me you can't get over old prejudices! I don't want to hear you saying, "You know, I'm just that way. I've just been that way all my life. I've just had a hard time loving a certain color in people."

Don't give me that, Jack, because the Word of God says it won't wash!

"Well, you know," some will say, "I'm from the old school."

Really? Don't you think it's about time to graduate?

I know the name of that "old school," because I took some classes there, too. It's called Flesh University! You can rename sin anything you want, but it's still sin. It's time we stopped making excuses. It's time we stopped throwing up a smoke screen of "tradition" and started being obedient to God's Word.

Growing up in Alabama, I learned to hate white people at an early age. My uncle, the only person in my family that I really respected, had taught me that the only good white person was a dead white person. He *I learned to hate* used to tell me, "Look, Ken, you've got three *white people* things against you. Number one, you're black *at an* and you live in America. Number two, you're *early age.* going to have to be three times better than any white person to get the same opportunities. And number three, you are a black who was born and raised in Alabama—in the deep South. You can't trust any white person."

I grew up with this. And the only reason I went out for football (I was a better baseball player) was so I could legally hurt white people. But after I came to Christ in high school, life began to change for me—dramatically. Now here I am *married* to a white lady and pastoring a church that's 60 to 70 percent white. Don't even try to tell me that God doesn't change people in the power of His Holy Spirit!

WHO SAID YOU WERE SUPPOSED TO BE COMFORTABLE?

When we founded Antioch Bible Church here on the east side of Seattle, we wanted a church for *all* people. And even though we know that goal is biblical, frankly, it isn't always comfortable.

That's okay.

Do you realize the Bible never says that church is supposed to be "comfortable" or "easy"? That's our idea, not God's. As a matter of fact, as you read the book of Acts, you can see how the Spirit of God continually worked to keep the believers *uncomfortable.* They were never allowed to settle into a warm, familiar rut. From the time they left that stuffy upper room after Pentecost, the thrust was always outward.

The only reason I went out for football was so I could legally hurt white people.

There's no doubt about it, though, when you walk into a worship service at Antioch Bible Church, you've got to claim Philippians 2. No matter what flavor of humanity you may be—black, white, Asian, Hispanic—when you walk in, there may be some music bouncing off the walls that doesn't caress your worshipful ecstasy.

What do I mean by claiming Philippians 2? Listen to this:

> Fulfill my joy by being like-minded, having the same love, being of one accord, of one mind. Let nothing be done through selfish ambition or conceit, but in lowliness of mind let each esteem others better than himself. Let each of you look out not only for his own interests, but also for the interests of others. Let this mind be in you which was also in Christ Jesus... (Philippians 2:2–5, NKJV).

You might walk into our worship center on a Sunday morning, hear the music, and say, "Oh no, not *that* again!"

But at that very moment, you're going against the spirit of Scripture (Or maybe I should say the Spirit of God). What kind of attitude do you have? You ought to walk in and say, "Wow, that's not my favorite style of worship, but I know it must be a real delight and a blessing to some of the other folks here. So I get to praise God today because someone else—my brother, my sister— is being ministered to and prepared to hear the Word of God. Me?

I've got to be more mature today and get myself ready to worship with them." The following week, those people who were enjoying last week's music so much will have to deal with music that really blesses you, but doesn't bless them at all! And *they* will have to claim Philippians 2 and praise God that you are being ministered to.

That's the church.

That's "esteeming others better than yourself."

That's what being part of a big, diverse family is all about.

OUR OWN KIND?

I believe Acts 8–13 is the apex of what the church should be like in the New Testament. For instance, if you look at the church at Antioch, up in Syria, you see different races and nationalities and cultures melded together into a giving, ministering, caring, accepting, sending body.

No wonder folks in that city started calling them "little Christs." It was probably meant to be an insult, but it wasn't!

Now if the Lord in His wisdom has given us the book of Acts as a model to see what He intended the church to look like, then it follows that churches should resemble that pattern today. After studying for years the New Testament and the book of Acts, I've come to the conclusion that the church today doesn't much look like the church in Acts.

Now if it doesn't, where did the change come from? Why did the church cease to be and look like the New Testament church?

It's really no great mystery. Through the years I believe we've become caught up in what man's ideas of the church ought to be, instead of making the church line up with God's Word. And I'm here to tell you now that if you have an all-black church, or an all-white church, or an all-Korean church, or any all-racial church, it's not the biblical pattern.

I like to put these things out in a straightforward way so that you don't have to wonder what I believe. I don't want you setting down this book and saying, "Now I wonder what Hutch *really* thinks about this issue?"

For my part, I do not believe the Bible is at all vague or confusing about what the church should look like. When the very first "cross-cultural" murmuring arose between the Greek and Hebrew widows in Acts 6, what did they do? Have a church split? Did they found the First Church of the Greek Gospel across town, so that all the Greek-speaking folks could be more comfortable with "their own kind"? Not on your life! They appointed wise, Spirit-filled men to wrestle with the issues on the table and deal with the problem. *Boom!* They dealt with it, and the church went right on growing.

We've become comfortable with a certain set of traditions and color scheme.

Why do we have all of these all-black, all-white, all-minority churches today? Because we have swallowed a lie in society. Society tells us when things get a little rough, we ought to make it easy on ourselves by dividing. We start making excuses for not looking the way God wants us to look. And the biggest excuse has been, "Well you know, we're just comfortable around our own kind!"

You've heard that, haven't you?

It's a flat-out lie.

Do you know why I know it's a lie? Because men and women marry! Like the book title says, women are from Venus and men are from Mars, but guess what? They keep getting together. And if you're more comfortable "around your own kind," I've got to write a different book for you!

The truth is, we have become comfortable and at ease with a certain style, a certain set of traditions, and a certain color scheme in our congregation. It pleases us to be with people of the same culture, same politics, and same income level. The church has developed in this way because we have not accepted God's command to put other people's needs above our own.

How would today's church have solved the problem in Acts 6? We'd have probably set up a first service for the Greek-speakers and a second service for the Hebrew-speakers. We'd give them each their own languages, traditions, music, and ethnic refreshments. And then we'd say, "Wow, aren't we unified? Aren't we working together! We may never actually *see* one another, but we never fight, either!"

Isn't that what we see being done with music in today's church? We have a "contemporary service" for one group of people and then a "traditional service" catering to another group of people. And by doing that, we never have to feel stretched or challenged or uncomfortable by someone else's dress, worship style, or music tastes. We get to be with our "own kind" and have a service that pleases us and makes us feel relaxed and comfortable.

We supposedly "unify" by further dividing ourselves!

We supposedly "unify" by further dividing ourselves! How unbiblical can we get? How will we ever learn to accept one another's differences in the power of the Holy Spirit? How will we ever learn to put others' needs and interests above our own?

What are we going to do when we get to heaven? Head over for the uptight white traditional side? Edge our way over to the black soul-brother side? Get comfortable with a big crowd of Chinese? No, we'll *all* be around the throne, praising Him together with one voice.

Seems to me we ought to be getting warmed up while we're still down here.

PAUL GETS THE BIG PICTURE

But the Lord said unto [Ananias], Go thy way, for [Saul] is
a chosen vessel unto me, to bear my name before the Gentiles, and kings, and the children of Israel; for I will show
him how great things he must suffer for my name's sake
(9:15–16).

The Lord was expecting a big, quick learning curve from Saul of
Tarsus.

It wasn't going to be easy. It was never *meant* to be easy.

The Lord was explaining to Ananias, "Here's how it works. I'm
going to call Paul out of his comfort zone to get him into someone else's comfort zone, so that he can teach them how to get out
of their comfort zone to get into someone else's comfort zone."
And so on and so on! That is the church.

By the way, how long has it been since you stepped out of
your comfort zone?

The Lord was saying, "Where am I going to send you, Paul?
I'm going to start with those who are the lowest of the low in your
eyes…the Gentiles. Then I'm going to put you before kings and
nobility…the highest of the high. And I'm also going to send you
to your own people, who will be the toughest audience of all!"

The church is supposed to be for the lowest of the low and the
highest of the high (according to the world's standards). And it's
also for those religious types who think they know the truth but,
in fact, may not know it at all. So the church is for the
unchurched, and the church is for the churched. The church is
for those who are poor and disregarded in society and for those
who are wealthy and influential.

But when you walk in the church door there's no difference.

That's what the church is supposed to be like.

Are you with me? Are you still glad you bought this book? Let me see if I can attack this subject from another angle.

In Acts 8, God allowed persecution to come into the church, and the believers dispersed. Right off the bat, He sent Philip to Samaria.

Boom! So now you've got Jews and Samaritans in the church—two groups who had been highly prejudiced toward one another and hated each other on sight. Now that's a start! But He wasn't through yet.

Then He turned around and sent Philip out of Samaria and along a desert road on the way to Gaza, where he met an Ethiopian. Not surprisingly, Philip rolled up his sleeves and led the Ethiopian to the Lord.

Boom! Now you've got Jews in the church, Samaritans in the church, and Africans in the church.

And then the Lord ambushes Saul—a man who hated the church—on the way to Damascus. Saul accepts Jesus Christ and gets his name changed to Paul.

Boom! Now you've got Jews in the church, Samaritans in the church, Africans in the church, and former persecutors in the church.

Not long after Paul's conversion, the Lord sends Peter—Mr. Jewish Purity—to preach the gospel to Cornelius, a God-fearing Roman centurion.

Boom! Now you've got Jews, Samaritans, Africans, former persecutors, and Gentiles in the church. And as the gospel rolled out farther and farther across the world, more and more peoples and nationalities and races joined God's growing family.

Now...will you tell me what the church is supposed to look like today?

Many people say to me, "Hutcherson, you've just got an agenda." What they mean is that I've got an agenda because I'm black. You bet I've got an agenda! But it's not because I'm black, it's because I'm a Christian who believes in the Word of God. That's my agenda. You see, when I became a Christian back in 1969, that fact overrode my blackness. It overrode my likes, my dislikes, my upbringing, and my comfort zones. I'm just as black as ever, but I've got to line up with the Word even if it overrides my culture and the way I was raised.

When I became a Christian, that fact overrode my blackness.

When the Word tells me to do something, I have no excuse but to be obedient, whether it's comfortable or not. That's what the church is all about, being obedient to the Word of God and loving my brothers and sisters in such a way that the world might know that there is a God in our midst!

THE CHURCH IN A SHEET

[Peter] fell into a trance, and saw heaven opened, and a certain vessel descending unto him, as it had been a great sheet knit at the four corners, and let down to the earth; in which were all manner of four-footed beasts of the earth, and wild beasts, and creeping things, and fowls of the air. And there came a voice to him, Rise, Peter, kill, and eat. But Peter said, Not so, Lord..." (10:10–14).

Contradiction! You can't say "No, Lord!" Those words just don't go together.

"Peter, kill and eat."

"No, nada, can't do it, never have done it. I'm a good Jewish believer."

"Peter, you *will* do it, because it's transition time. I'm moving away from the old and into the new. If you don't obey, you'll get left behind!"

Do you know what I think the sheet in Peter's vision represents? The church. I think the Lord was saying to him, "Peter, here is a picture of the church, clean and unclean people, common and uncommon, men and women from different backgrounds and cultures and traditions. Here is the new way it's going to be, Peter. Don't you ever say that someone I have made clean is not clean. Don't you say that to me, Peter. I am Christ, I have cleansed them, and they *are* clean."

I have no excuse but to be obedient to the Word... whether it's comfortable or not.

The message of the vision wasn't about eating, it was about the church.

Christ was preparing His man for what was to come. Did you notice that when the vision was finished, the sheet rose back into heaven? Do you know what that means? What it means is, "Peter, the church age, this whole new way—it's temporary. When I get through with this brief age of grace, I'm going to take My church away at the rapture and bring it into heaven."

While Peter thought on the vision, the Spirit said unto him, Behold, three men seek thee. Arise, therefore, and get thee down, and go with them, doubting nothing (10:19–20).

The church isn't made to be comfortable with "my kind of people."

Wow! And some people think God doesn't move very fast! He didn't give Peter any time at all to process this whole transition. He just said, "Get up, Peter, there are three Gentiles knocking on your door. Get ready to go with them!"

Peter said something like, "Fine, Lord, but

I'm hungry. Can't I have these guys in for some lunch first?"

God expected Peter to obey promptly. To set aside his lifelong prejudice immediately. Was it *comfortable* for Peter to have lunch with these Gentiles? Probably not. But God didn't expect Peter's comfort; He expected Peter's obedience.

*Comfortable?
Cozy?
Easy?
Not on your life.
We're talking
about His way,
not ours.*

It really doesn't matter how much you like certain people or don't like certain people. It doesn't matter if you appreciate certain styles and customs or feel turned off by those styles and customs. It doesn't matter. There are all kinds of people in that big sheet, and if Christ has called them "clean," then you've got to deal with it...or get left behind in His plan and purpose and will.

Listen, the church isn't made to sit around and be comfortable with "my kind of people" or "my kind of money" or "my kind of lack of it" or "my kind of color" or "my kind of education."

The church is for all people. It's for us to blend in together so when someone walks in they see Jesus living there.

Comfortable? No.

Cozy? No.

Easy? Not on your life.

But we're talking about His way, not ours.

CONSTRUCTION ZONE

The church is supposed to be a place where you can come and find out what God wants you to do. It's a construction zone, where lives are being built and rebuilt to the glory of God. For that reason, it is not a place where you're going to come and expect to "feel good" all the time.

If you haven't been lining up with God's Word through the previous week, the worship and the preaching ought to make you a little sad. Maybe even miserable. If you haven't been in fellowship with Christ, you ought to feel very uncomfortable—until you get things squared away with Him and His people.

If you *never* feel uncomfortable in church, there are two probable options: you've either done a good job preparing your heart for Sunday morning or your pastor isn't declaring the undiluted Word of God. In so many churches today, men and women walk through the door after living all week any way they please. And they walk out after the service unfazed—not even feeling convicted about their unholy lifestyle. That's not the church, friend, that's a social club with a steeple.

The true church of Jesus Christ will get in your face. It will say, "Yes, you're doing some good things in your life, but regardless of your noble efforts, you're not going to make it to heaven or accomplish anything of eternal value in your life if you don't know Jesus Christ." And it says to believers, "Yes, you did well to accept Christ as Savior. That's the first step. But the journey is more than one step! You need to keep walking in the Spirit. You need to grow more Christlike every day of your life."

As the book of Hebrews puts it, we need to "exhort one another daily, while it is called Today, lest any of you be hardened through the deceitfulness of sin" (Hebrews 3:13). In the church of Jesus Christ, we encourage and challenge one another to live holy and godly lives and fight free from the entangling thorns of sin.

That's not always comfortable.

We shouldn't expect it to be.

Because
We Aren't
Bold in
Our Witness

[The Sanhedrin] conferred among themselves, saying, What shall we do to these men? For that indeed a notable miracle hath been done by them is manifest to all those who dwell in Jerusalem; and we cannot deny it. But that it spread no further among the people, let us threaten them, that they speak henceforth to no man in this name. And they called them, and commanded them not to speak at all nor teach in the name of Jesus (4:15–18).

We can all see what happened in this passage of Scripture, this account of the first persecution. But what *didn't* happen?

The Sanhedrin didn't command Peter and John to stop *speaking*. Evidently that wasn't the issue.

They didn't order them to stop *teaching*. That wasn't the issue.

They didn't even say, "You can't talk to the people about God." That wasn't the issue, either.

The issue was the name of Jesus Christ.

"We warn you, don't speak anymore in *that name!* Don't teach anymore in *that name!* If you do, we're going to make you very, very sorry."

When you think about it, Satan can put up with lots of religion. It doesn't really bother him; he can even get into religion himself.

He can put on robes and do incense. He can put on a suit and preach love and good works. He can slick back his hair, go on TV and do a phony healing service. Scripture says that he "disguises himself as an angel of light" (2 Corinthians 11:14, NASB).

Satan can endure any amount of "God talk"; it may not be comfortable to him, but he can endure it, because it presents no real danger to him or his plans. But when you start talking about the *Lord Jesus Christ,* you'd better strap on your helmet, because you just joined the war. You're in for the battle of your lives, and hell will oppose you with all the means at its disposal.

The rulers of Israel had a big problem with the healing of the lame man at the Beautiful Gate. They couldn't deny it—there were too many eyewitnesses! So they said to each other, "How can we fight this? We can't deny this thing. Let's just nail them for teaching in the name of Jesus. Because if we can eliminate them teaching Jesus, we've got them! Why, oh, why can't we keep this Man in the grave? We thought our problems were over when we put Him on that cross!"

The greatest compliment someone can give you is to say you're an extremist for Jesus.

Isn't it the same way in the world today? The issue is the name of Jesus. When I first started playing pro ball my teammates would tell me, "Watch out when you give your interviews, Hutch, because if you talk about Jesus, they won't come back to interview you anymore."

And I thought to myself, "So what? I'll at least get ONE good interview, and I'll make sure I talk about Jesus!" After that, of course, word got around and the reporters avoided me in the locker room. (To tell the truth, it was kind of peaceful.) When I had made an especially good play, they'd go over and talk to one of my teammates. "Boy, Hutcherson made quite a play on that third and three, didn't he? He really stuffed that guy."

And my teammates would answer, "Well, why don't you ask *him* about it?"

It's funny how that works. If I would step up to the mike and say, "You know, I'd really like to give the glory to God," the media might flinch, but no one would be that offended. They'd say, "Ooh, there's an angle for a story. He's a moral kind of guy. He believes in God."

Or I could say, "I'm a *religious* person and I don't believe in doing this or that." That impresses them, too. They might even write a few lines about it. No one's offended when you talk about religion or ethics or even God. You can tell about being a Buddhist, or a Moslem, or a Mormon, or a New Age crystal-gazer, and everything's cool.

But when you say, "Yes, I want to thank my Lord and my Savior Jesus Christ," the interview's over, Jack! Cut it, cut it! Whenever you make it personal and bring up the name of Jesus, folks say, "Ah, you guys on the religious right are a bunch of nuts! You want to force everyone to think the same way you do."

When they respond to you like that, do you know what you should do? You should smile and tell them thank you. Why? Because the greatest compliment someone can give you is to say you're an extremist for Jesus. When that happens, the angels in heaven look over the edge and take notice. When you think about it, what better thing could you be known for? "He loves Jesus! She's a total Jesus freak!" Isn't that better than people saying, "He's in love with himself" or "She's stuck on herself"?

If you're going to be a fool, it might as well be for Christ. He is our life!

Let me ask you a question. When someone close to you—a friend or a family member—starts walking with God and trusting God and speaking boldly for God, are you bumped out of your comfort zone? Are you just a little embarrassed? Maybe you're like those old Brylcream hair tonic commercials where they sang, "A little dab'll do ya." Maybe you think it's okay to have just a dab or two of Christianity in the right places, but don't overdo it or people will think you're a religious nut.

I want to go on record here and now that I don't mind being a nut for Christ. I'm double nutty. I'm triple nutty. I'm a macadamia nut. I'm dry-roasted! It doesn't really matter what kind of nut you think I am. The way I figure it, if you're going to be a fool for something, it might as well be for Christ, because *He is our very life.* Without Him, I'd be worse than a nut; I'd be lost!

I like how Paul handled that issue when he was on trial in front of Governor Festus and King Agrippa. When he was in the middle of declaring the Resurrection, the Roman governor started shouting in his face: "Paul, thou art beside thyself; much learning doth make thee mad" (Acts 26:24). Or, to translate the passage into the Hutcherson International Version, "Paul, you're a double-nut sundae! You're out in the ozone, man!"

And Paul came back with these words:

"I am not mad…but speak the words of truth and reason.… I would to God that not only you, but also all who hear me today, might become both almost and altogether such as I am, except for these chains" (26:25, 29, NKJV).

In other words, "I'm not really crazy at all, you just think I am. But crazy or not, I wish you could be just like me and know Jesus Christ the way I do!"

The world is certainly nutty over what they believe in. I knew a guy who wouldn't walk out of his house without first consulting his horoscope. (And they call me stupid for being excited about the Lord!)

What are you known for in your circle of friends and acquaintances and associates? Are you known as a person who is zealous for Jesus? Maybe a little bit over the edge? That's a badge of honor!

Throughout my pro football career, I got picked on more as a Christian than I ever did as a rookie. I always took it as a great compliment. It meant more to me than a write-up on the front page of the sports section.

> And they called them, and commanded them not to speak
> at all nor teach in the name of Jesus (4:18).

Right. Like that's really going to rock someone who has sold out to Jesus Christ! If you've met Jesus, if you've walked with Jesus, if you've soaked up His presence and tasted His power in your life, a threat like that doesn't do anything to slow you down. It just makes you more sure than ever that you're on the right track.

TWO WAYS TO SHUT YOU UP

> Now when they saw the boldness of Peter and John, and
> perceived that they were uneducated and untrained men,
> they marveled (4:13, NKJV).

One of the first things your enemies will do to counter your boldness is to treat you with a condescending attitude. They'll talk down to you. They'll shake their heads and roll their eyes. They'll wave you off or laugh up their sleeves. They'll act superior and look down their noses at you. Their aim is to make you feel embarrassed or ashamed, as if you've done something foolish or bush-league for being excited about Jesus. They want you to feel badly about what you believe.

When I first came over to the Seahawks from the Dallas Cowboys, I wore a T-shirt with these words on it: *Hutch is going to*

Seattle to do God's battle! I had all these great Christian T-shirts. So when I walked into the locker room or the training room, some of my new teammates were looking at each other and thinking, This Hutch guy is a little goofy. But I made them respect me out on the field. They may have thought I was goofy, but I did my job!

"You come up to my room. I'm on some stuff called Jerusalem Gunjee."

During the first training camp when no one on the team knew me, they thought something was going on because I laughed so much and had such a good time. They were saying to each other, "He says he's a Christian, but there's something else going on here, too. Ain't no way in the world anybody can be that happy all the time. He must be on something."

So a couple of the guys came to me after practice one afternoon and said, "Hutch, c'mon man, be honest with us. What are you on?"

I said, "What?"

"Oh man," they said, "we know you're on somethin', man. Are you gonna tell us or not?"

"Okay," I said, looking around. "I guess you guys got me figured out. You come up to my room later on tonight, man. I'm on some stuff called 'Jerusalem Gunjee.' This stuff is over 2,000 years old. It'll just blow your mind. So after curfew tonight—after they check all the rooms—y'all come on down to my room and I'll share wit'cha."

So sure enough, about quarter to twelve that night, I hear footsteps in the hall and a tapping on my door. Someone outside was whispering, "Hey Hutch, open up, man. It's us."

I said, "C'mon in. Sit down. I've got the stuff, and it's hot. It'll knock you over."

So they sat down, their eyes open wide. I pulled open my

drawer and pulled my Bible out and said, "Here it is right here!"

They said, "You're nuts, man! You're crazy!"

"I may be nuts and crazy," I said, "but you're the guys who are sneaking around the halls at midnight 'cause you think I'm on something!"

If mockery and taunting don't work to get through to you, your enemies may play hardball. They'll come after you with threats and intimidation. They'll tell you to shut up and try to make it stick. This is a method that's worked pretty well for them in our country. They've shut up Christians at universities. They've shut up Christians in public schools. They've shut up Christians in the workplace.

We believers have become very thin-skinned. We don't like to be threatened. We shy away from confrontations. We get our feelings hurt when we're frowned at or ripped in the media, and we find ourselves thinking, "I'm such a nice person…I don't know why people don't like me!"

It's true, one reason they might not like you is simply because you're not a very likable, attractive person. People who behave like selfish jerks tend to get treated like selfish jerks. It's the law of the jungle. But if you've been bold and humble and consistent in your witness, chances are what they won't like about you is *Jesus*.

We believers have become very thin-skinned.

They didn't like Him two thousand years ago when He walked among us. They don't like Him now.

They didn't want Him around then. They don't want Him around now.

They took hold of Him and killed Him then. They'd do the same now if they had the chance.

And if you deliberately and publicly associate your name with His, they won't like you, either. You'll take some heat. Count on it. Don't be shocked and surprised when it happens. Peter wrote: "Beloved, think it not strange concerning the fiery trial which is to test you, as though some strange thing happened unto you" (1 Peter 4:12).

It's not strange at all. The only reason it might seem strange to you is because you haven't been paying attention to the Word of God. Did you ever think of those insults and cold-shoulder treatments as blessings? Listen to what Scripture says:

> Blessed are you when they revile and persecute you, and say all kinds of evil against you falsely for My sake. Rejoice and be exceedingly glad, for great is your reward in heaven, for so they persecuted the prophets who were before you (Matthew 5:11–12, NKJV).

Exceedingly glad! Hilariously glad! Doing backflips glad! The greatest blessing in all the world is to have the right people dislike you. It's time we started counting these slights, slurs, and put-downs as compliments! And if no one ever says anything negative about us, maybe *that's* the time when we should begin to worry. If we're no offense to the world, they probably don't even associate us with the name of Jesus. We're no threat to them at all.

> But Peter and John answered and said to them, "Whether it is right in the sight of God to listen to you more than to God, you judge. For we cannot but speak the things which we have seen and heard" (Acts 4:19, NKJV).

Now remember, this was the Sanhedrin, the supreme court of their day. There was no higher court in the land or in the *world* as far as the Jews were concerned. These were the seventy top leaders of Israel, with one high priest. They supposedly knew the Law better than anyone else. And here came these ignorant, unlearned men who just busted those guys in their own game!

Peter and John look up at them and say, "Well, your honors, you're the ones who are supposed to teach all the people how to glorify God. That's *your* job, O great Sanhedrin. So may we poor, unlearned fish jockeys ask you a question? If we walked into this room and told you, 'We want you to do thus and so,' but God says, 'No, I want you to do something else,' which should you do?"

Gotcha! The Sanhedrin must have sat there puffing and spluttering in their beards.

"Come on, Sanhedrin, who wants to answer first? If God tells us to do one thing, but we want to do another thing, which way should we go?"

The Sanhedrin, of course, would have to answer, "Obey God." And Peter and John said, "Well, that's just what we intend to do. We're going to do what God asks us to do. We would rather displease you than displease Him. We'd rather face punishment from you than discipline from Him."

> For we cannot but speak the things which we have seen and heard (4:20).

Peter and John were saying, "We're not talking about second-hand stuff here. We saw with our own eyes, we heard with our own ears." Later on Peter would write, "We have not followed cunningly devised fables when we made known unto you the power and coming of our Lord Jesus Christ, but were eyewitnesses of his majesty" (2 Peter 1:16).

Can't you just hear these guys? "We're talking about face-to-face encounters with the Son of God after you killed Him and He was raised from the dead. Now He is our God and King, reigning in heaven, and if you guys had any sense at all, you'd be jumping over to our side! Even if you kill us, you've already proven that doesn't stop anything!"

ARE WE DENYING CHRIST?

So when they had further threatened them, they let them go, finding nothing how they might punish them, because of the people; for all men glorified God for that which was done (4:21).

What did the Sanhedrin want out of that friendly little chat with Peter and John? They wanted to intimidate these disciples into denying the name of Christ. But the boys said, "No way. You're asking us to do the impossible. How can we deny what we've seen and heard? How can we deny what's happened in our lives? This is Reality with a capital *R*, and we're not going to sweep it under the rug because *you* say so."

"This is Reality with a capital R, *and we're not going to sweep it under the rug."*

Here's my question: In what ways are you and I denying Christ? We may not find ourselves in a situation just like this one, where we're actually on trial for teaching Christ in public (At least not yet). But there are other ways to deny Him, aren't there? There are other "more acceptable" ways to lose our boldness and deny the presence and power of Jesus Christ in our lives.

It's one thing to have a bold witness when everything is sunshine and roses in your life. But are you singing the same tune when your roof falls in? When your spouse gets sick? When your kid gets in trouble? When your job gets downsized? Don't tell me that people around you aren't watching!

Do you deny that He can work within your "impossible" situation?

- Maybe you're in a difficult marriage. You've been deeply frustrated and hurt by the attitude and behavior of your spouse. Are you denying that God has the power to work in that man or woman's heart, and in your marriage? Have you thrown in the towel? Do other people see you in despair, even giving up on God?
- Maybe you're in some deep financial straits. Are you denying Christ the ability to walk with you through this situation and bring you out of debt as you trust Him and follow the principles of His Word?
- Maybe you're denying that God can change you, even if He decides not to change your present circumstances. You're denying that He can so change your heart and your attitude that your circumstances just won't matter anymore.

When I think about God changing someone I thought could never change, I think about a close friend I had in the NFL. We were so close that I even named one of my sons after him. When we first met, he was one of the most self-absorbed, self-reliant, hard-exteriored persons I have ever met. He was Mr. Positive Thinking. Mr. I-can-do-anything.

I remember thinking to myself, This guy will NEVER, EVER change. Nothing gets to him. Nothing shakes him. Even when he was having problems in his marriage, his attitude was, "Hey, this is the way I am. If she doesn't like it, that's the way it goes."

I remember him saying, "I will *never* be a Christian. I don't need your God. I will never change. This is the way I am, so forget talking to me about it."

But do you know what? He kept watching my life. He kept watching the lives of a couple other Christian guys on our football team. He listened to our witness, even though it bugged him. And even though this strong man resisted with all his strength, he knew there was something about Christ in a man's life that he couldn't explain away. Even with all his positive thinking, he couldn't get past the idea of being "limited." He hated to think about the fact that he couldn't be all-sufficient.

I used to say to him, "You know, I can have all the positive thinking I want. But will that enable me to cover Cliff Branch tomorrow?" (Branch was a wide receiver for the Oakland Raiders and seemed to be a scoring threat on about every play from scrimmage.)

I said, "You know and I know that all of my positive thinking will only carry me as far as my abilities. There's got to be something beyond our human abilities to help us cope with life, man."

That really bothered him. He hated the idea of being limited. But he kept thinking about what I'd said. And when God finally broke this man, He really broke him. He threw his life wide open to Jesus Christ and accepted Him as Savior and Lord. He gave his life to the only One who could never be limited by anything.

And now this guy is beyond a doubt one of the strongest, most uncompromising believers I have ever seen in my life. What a lesson that was for me! Don't ever give up on someone who you'd thought would "never accept Christ" or "never change." When you do that, you are limiting God to how far you can see…how much you can believe.

Don't ever doubt that people are watching your life. And some of the people who are watching you most closely may be those you thought would "never be interested."

Our message is a little mixed-up in the church today. We think we are supposed to be telling people what we've done for

God. But people could care less what you've done for God. That's no big deal at all. That won't ring anyone's chimes. What people want to know is, what has God done for you lately? How is He working in your life? How is He making a difference in you and in that "impossible" situation of yours? How is it that you can be under all that pressure and stress and still sing the glory of God?

I've always admired "tea kettle" Christians. They can be up to their neck in hot water and still sing! The world wants to know how this God you talk about makes a difference in your life *when you're sitting on the burner.* They want to see the reality of a life within you beyond anything they've ever experienced. Peter had it nailed pretty good when he wrote, "Be ready always to give an answer to every man that asketh you a reason of the hope that is in you" (1 Peter 3:15).

Don't ever doubt that people are watching your life.

Why would they ask you about your hope? Because it doesn't make earthly sense! When they see you holding on to your faith and joy in Christ in the middle of the storm, in the middle of the pressure and stress, they say to themselves, What's going on here? What's his secret? What's she got that I haven't got?

"Be ready always," the Word says. How do I get ready when I don't know what's coming? That's easy! I make sure that I'm filled with the Holy Spirit.

THE KEY TO BOLDNESS

And they were all filled with the Holy Spirit, and they spoke the word of God with boldness (4:31).

To be bold in our own strength is just being reckless. We'll just thrash around like a linebacker in a china shop. We'll do more damage than good. But to be bold in the Holy Spirit is to open a door for God's power to move into your situation. We desperately need the ministry of the Holy Spirit as believers today, because so many of us are missing that boldness—that holy courage in Christ that is not afraid to stand up for what the Word teaches.

The world isn't afraid at all to stand up for what *they* believe; have you noticed? The world is much more bold with their lack of morals than you and I as believers are with our morals. They don't mind letting you know what they believe and what they think—and don't much care if you like it or don't like it!

One of my Christian friends was on the beach recently when he saw a young man walking along in shorts and a T-shirt. And emblazoned across that T-shirt in bold letters were the words: STAMP OUT VIRGINITY!

My friend walked over to him and said, "Hey, nice shirt."

"Thanks," the young man said, "I like it."

"Would you do me a favor?" my friend asked.

"Well—if I can."

"I want you to go home and I want you to pull that T-shirt off. Then I want you to wash it, fold it up, and put it in your drawer and keep it. Are you married? No? Well, when you do get married and you have your first daughter, on her first date pull out that T-shirt and give it to the boy who's taking her out!"

It gave the young man a fresh perspective! My friend's message was bold—but no more bold than the message on that T-shirt.

Listen, friend, we need to be bold! Life's too short to play patty-cake. The world has had enough and more than enough of wishy-washy, namby-pamby, hand-wringing Christianity. Those days are over! Are we evangelicals or evanjellyfish, with no spiritual vertebrae? What does it matter if the world thinks we're stupid? We'll just be more stupid for Christ. What does it matter if people think we're fools? We'll just become more foolish for Christ.

The key is in allowing the Holy Spirit to control your life. How long has it been—be honest, now—since you prayed for boldness? How long has it been since you asked the Spirit of God to so fill you up so that you would be absolutely *fearless* in your witness for Him?

You say, "Hutch, that's just not me."

No, it isn't *you*. That's the point. You need Him.

STEPHEN TELLS 'EM STRAIGHT

They stirred up the people, and the elders, and the scribes, and came upon [Stephen], and caught him, and brought him to the council, and set up false witnesses, who said, This man ceaseth not to speak blasphemous words against this holy place, and the law.... And all that sat in the council, looking steadfastly on him, saw his face as it had been the face of an angel.

Then said the high priest, Are these things so? (6:12–13, 15; 7:1).

Stephen, on trial for his life, was accused of three phony, trumped-up charges. It's the oldest trick in the book. If you can't find anything wrong with a person, pay someone to lie about him so you can put an end to him.

Stephen, full of the Holy Spirit, blew off the counterfeit charges and took the opportunity by storm, launching into a guided history of the Jewish people. He walked them through Genesis and Exodus, did a flyby over 1 and 2 Samuel, touched down briefly in 1 Kings, then hopped over into Isaiah, before plunging them right into the book of Acts.

Now, all that Old Testament Scripture just set them up. But

when he took them into the book of Acts, that got him killed.

They did not want to hear the truth. They could not *bear* to hear the truth. Dr. Luke, the author, describes the scene with his usual eye for detail:

> When they heard these things, they were cut to the heart, and they gnashed on him with their teeth.... Then they cried out with a loud voice, and stopped their ears, and ran upon him with one accord (7:54, 57).

Stephen preached the Word of God, and he wasn't afraid to apply it. Not even when it hurt. Not even when his listeners were boiling mad. But today, we're afraid of that kind of boldness. People will say to the pastor, "You know, Pastor, what you're saying is true enough, but you've got to be more *sensitive* to how other people feel. You're kind of forward, Pastor. Maybe you should pull it back a little bit. You've got to let people have an opportunity to come around themselves." That may be, but then, how do I know if the people to whom I'm speaking will have another opportunity to respond to God's Word? How do I know there will be a tomorrow for them—or me? That's the weakness, I believe, with some of the popular "friendship evangelism" approaches. We may concentrate so much on the friendship we don't get around to the evangelism! And Scripture makes it clear that we're to make the most of every opportunity, because the days are evil (see Ephesians 5:16). *Today* is the day of salvation; yesterday and tomorrow don't even exist!

The bottom line: We'd better be bold when the Lord gives us an opportunity.

I know Stephen truly believed this, because my boy didn't

How do I know there will be a tomorrow for them— or me?

bite his tongue! He declared the Word, he applied it to the situation, and—before he knew it—he was standing before his Lord in heaven getting a high-five and a big hug. Now that's not such a bad outcome!

DELIVERING THE GOODS

But when they departed from Perga, they came to Antioch in Pisidia, and went into the synagogue on the sabbath day, and sat down. And after the reading of the law and the prophets the rulers of the synagogue sent unto them, saying, Ye men and brethren, if ye have any word of exhortation for the people, say on. Then Paul stood up, and beckoning with his hand said, Men of Israel, and ye that fear God, listen... (13:14–16).

Barnabas had taken Paul under his wing, sponsoring and encouraging this former persecutor of the church. But now it was time to hit the streets. Now it was time to deliver the goods. The Holy Spirit sent them off on their first missionary journey, and it was time for the encouraging time to take a backseat to the teaching time.

Paul gave them the Word in Antioch, Pisidia. What was the message? As with Peter and Stephen before him, he walked them through a brief history of the Jewish nation. And then he brought them down to the point: Messiah, Jesus Christ, has answered all their history. Paul laid Jesus' life on them: what He did and how He died and that three days later he was resurrected. And then he brought them to this all-important focus: What are you going to do with the information I've given you? Are you going to reject this, and suffer the consequences?

"Therefore let it be known to you, brethren, that through this Man is preached to you the forgiveness of sins; and by

Him everyone who believes is justified from all things from which you could not be justified by the law of Moses. Beware therefore, lest what has been spoken in the prophets come upon you: 'Behold, you despisers, marvel and perish! For I work a work in your days, a work which you will by no means believe, though one were to declare it to you'" (13:38–41, NKJV).

Paul laid it out and gave an invitation the very first time he set foot in Antioch of Pisidia. And I'd like you to notice something. He didn't take fifteen years to learn their customs. He didn't do a six-month study to find out their cultural sensitivities. He just preached the gospel, straight out.

Make sure that when you have an opportunity, whether with one person or a thousand, you give witness to Jesus Christ. That doesn't mean preach a sermon or go through a sixteen-page booklet with little diagrams in it. It just means that you give a first-person account of what Christ has meant to your life and offer the opportunity for the person to receive Jesus Christ as Savior.

Now, if I met you and got acquainted with you on some occasion, it would be great to become your friend. If the opportunity was there, that would be fantastic. A man can't have too many good friends. But do you know something? God is not going to hold me accountable for making friends with you, as pleasant and as desirable as that might be. He's going to hold me accountable for bearing witness of the Good News to you.

How do I know if I'll have three hours or three days or three months to build a friendship with you? How do I know you won't step out in the street and get hit by a bus? It happens to the best of us!

> But when the Jews saw the multitudes, they were filled with envy, and spoke against those things which were spoken by Paul, contradicting and blaspheming (13:45).

Ouch! What's happening here? We've got some conflict going on! People are getting upset! Hey, is thing going sour, or what? What would Paul and Barnabas do? They might have got together and said, "Ooh. Maybe we should rethink our presentation. Maybe we should back off a little bit. We're making too many people mad. They don't want to listen anymore, so let's come back and be humble. Let's soften our message a little so we can be friends."

The gospel of Jesus is cross-cultural by its very nature.

Is that what they said? No! The more angry the people in the city became, the bolder those missionaries became. They just kept on preaching. They got bold, not humble.

> Then Paul and Barnabas grew bold, and said, It was necessary that the word of God should first have been spoken to you; but seeing ye put it from you, and judge yourselves unworthy of everlasting life, lo, we turn to the Gentiles.
>
> And when the Gentiles heard this, they were glad, and glorified the word of the Lord; and as many as were ordained to eternal life believed (13:46, 48).

There's a time to be humble, but not when people are getting mad at you for simply telling them the truth. *Be bold.* The church doesn't need to revamp its evangelism program because it offends somebody. We need to do it the way God tells us to do it, and leave the results with Him. We need to live in fear of God, not live in fear that we might transgress someone's cultural sensitivities. Let's face it, these days *whatever* you say will be offensive and politically incorrect to somebody. Every time you open your mouth in public you're going to "offend" somebody's sensibilities. So why make it complicated? Just give them the gospel. Lay it on them.

You see, the gospel of Jesus is cross-cultural by its very nature. It's African. It's European. It's Asian. It's Latin. It's Eskimo. It's male. It's female. It's for the insider and the outsider, the up-and-comer and the down-and-outer. It's for sinners. It's for saints. I don't have to learn to be "sensitive" to you to give you the gospel of Jesus, because it's *already* sensitive to you. Besides that, the name of Jesus and His cross will always be offensive to some people, no matter how carefully I tread, no matter how much cultural tip-toeing I do.

"But Hutch," you say, "what happens when they're so mad they're not going to listen to you anymore?" I'm glad you asked! Just check out Acts 13:50.

> But the Jews stirred up the devout and honorable women, and the chief men of the city, and raised persecution against Paul and Barnabas, and expelled them out of their borders.

How would we respond to that kind of situation today? We'd say, "Oh man, I can't believe it, I knew we should have backed off! Good night, we turned the whole city off! We're failures!"

But that's not true. God's plan for us is that we give them the gospel, love them as much as we can, keep the truth in front of them, and when they reject it, we turn around, shake the dust off our feet, and go find someone who is ready to listen. And there will always be those whom God has prepared to listen.

When the Jews of Antioch, Pisidia, rejected the gospel, there were other folks standing in line, excited and ready to receive God's Word and the offer of salvation. It will always be that way. Some will reject, others are so ripe for the gospel that they'll knock you over leaping into the kingdom.

You and I don't need to have a memorized presentation to boldly share Christ with people. We don't need to know every salvation verse in the Bible. We don't need to understand every aspect of theological debate. It's good and helpful to know some of those things, yes, but we don't need them.

You may not even be able to tell them exactly what the Bible says, but you can tell them what convinced *you* to believe. You can tell them what happened in your life. That's what being a witness is all about.

Every one of us has what it takes to bring someone who's not in the kingdom to the place we are in the kingdom. Have you seen a change in your life since you've accepted Christ? Then you can tell someone about that change. And when you get through, just close it off by inviting them to accept Jesus too.

"Hutch, I don't know if I could do that."

Yes, you can! Steal a line from Nike and *just do it!* Ask them, "Do you want to accept Christ? Good, let's get on the phone, and I'll find someone to help both of us!" You've got to close that transaction if you possibly can. If you don't, Satan may steal away the seed you just planted in ready soil.

You don't have to be smooth. You don't have to eloquent. You don't have to have a ton of information. But you do need to be filled with the Holy Spirit, and you do need to be bold.

Listen, a nonbeliever doesn't care what the Scripture says in Greek and Hebrew, they just want to know: Will this thing work for me? Is it going to change my life? Is it going to make my family better? Is it going to save my marriage? Is it going to pull me out of this stinking pit I'm in? Is it going to help me be a better dad or mom?

As representatives of the church of Jesus Christ, we've got the only message that brings life out of death, and we've got all the power in the world through God's indwelling Holy Spirit.

If *that* doesn't make you bold and lovingly aggressive, you need to spend a little more time on your knees!

BECAUSE WE AREN'T USING OUR GIFTS

CHAPTER 5

Has your wife or husband ever said to you, "We need to have a serious talk"?

Ouch! Just saying "We need to talk" in a flat tone of voice is scary enough. But when your spouse says, "We need a *serious* talk…" Well, it kind of gives you a little quiver in your liver, doesn't it?

You know, we don't get real excited about those moments in our lives where we have to take long, honest looks at ourselves. Most of us would rather avoid moments like that (We prefer short, dishonest looks at ourselves!).

The apostle James compares us to folks who take a glance in the mirror and hurry off on our way. We don't want a *long* look. We just content ourselves with a quick glance to make sure we don't have any spinach in our teeth or something gross going on (James 1:22–25).

As I look at the condition of the church today, I have to come to the conclusion that we aren't doing as well as we did in the early days. And what would the Lord of the church say to us if He sat us down for one of those long, serious talks? (You might get a pretty good idea by reading Revelation 2–3!) We might not *want* to hear what He thinks of us when He looks at us with those "eyes like a flame of fire."

The church is not in good shape today.

As we've looked into the book of Acts and compared what we see in that church with what we see today, we have to conclude that something's been lost along the way. When I think of where the church was and where it is now, it reminds me of my own body. Because I was a pro football player, you might see me today and think I look big and strong. You might say, "Whoo, look at him." But if you knew me in the prime of my career, and *then* looked at me now, you might say, "Wow, what happened to him?" I'm not the physical specimen I used to be; I'm probably not ready to suit up with the Seahawks this Monday night. (Give me a couple weeks.)

What happens if the church refuses to exercise the gifts of the Spirit? Nothing.

In the same way, when we look at the book of Acts we have to say, "Wow, what happened to the church? It doesn't look like it used to!" And I believe one of the areas where we've lost much of our ground is in the area of gifts of the Holy Spirit.

Why is this such a serious matter to the Lord? Because when the Lord departed from the earth, He left behind a way for the world to continue to see Him…through His church. That's why we call the church the "body of Christ." God intended that every quality of Jesus Christ should walk through your fellowship's doors on Sunday morning. His compassion. His care. His leadership. His teaching. His encouragement. His mercy. His generosity. It's all there, through the gifts distributed by the Holy Spirit. It is a picture, or portrait, of God's Son.

The church is to exalt and show forth Jesus Christ by allowing all of His qualities to live through us, through the power of the Spirit (and never in our own strength). When that happens, Jesus Himself said, "And I, if I be lifted up from the earth, will draw all men unto me" (John 12:32).

When Christ is lifted up, when the world truly sees Him for who He is—sees Him in all His beauty and might—people are *drawn* to Him. But what happens if the church refuses to walk in the Spirit and exercise the gifts of the Spirit? What happens if we're lazy or careless or apathetic about it all?

I'll tell you what happens...*nothing.*

Christ is not exalted. The members of His body are not helped. The weak are not strengthened. The grieving are not comforted. The sleepy are not challenged. The wandering are not rebuked. The confused are not directed. And all those discouraged, beaten-down men and women in this cold, uncaring world of ours are not drawn to the Savior.

In fact, that is the very tragedy we have before us today.

And it is a very serious matter to the Lord of the church.

THE SPIRIT GOES TO WORK

They were all with one accord in one place. And suddenly there came a sound from heaven like a rushing mighty wind... (2:1–2).

The day before Pentecost there was no church. The day after, it was full, it was moving, it was growing, and it was turning that society upside down and inside out. In short—and in short order—it was a force to be reckoned with!

That's how the Holy Spirit works. When the Holy Spirit enters your life, there's a change. We're not talking about just rearranging the furniture, we're talking about moving walls around—making the ceiling into the floor, and the floor into the ceiling. It's radical. It'll rattle your teeth. Don't tell me that you're "not sure" if you've become a Christian or not!

As a believer in Jesus Christ, whether new or used, you're

going to have fruit. I can't tell you what kind of fruit it will be, but it's going to show up. It may be itty-bitty raisins. It may be dried-up prunes. It may not be much more than humility and a deep conviction of your sins, to begin with. But you can count on change. You can count on a new force flowing through your life that's ready to go to war with the old nature.

When the Holy Spirit moves in, there are new abilities to love and serve one another; gifts of the Spirit for the common good and the glory of Christ. Paul explained it like this:

> There are diversities of gifts, but the same Spirit. There are differences of ministries, but the same Lord. And there are diversities of activities, but it is the same God who works all in all. But the manifestation of the Spirit is given to each one for the profit of all.... But one and the same Spirit works all these things, distributing to each one individually as He wills (1 Corinthians 12:4–7, 11, NKJV).

We've got different kinds of gifts from the Holy Spirit. We've got high-visibility gifts and we've got low-visibility gifts. Paul called it "diversities" in gifts. (The Holy Spirit believes in diversity!) A lot of us crave a high-visibility gift because it makes us look more important and prominent. It makes people think we're big time in the kingdom, and that we're tight with God. But is that gift more important than a low-visibility gift? No! These are simply different manifestations of the character of Christ, and the church needs them all, functioning in harmony, humming along like a well-tuned V-8.

Yes, the church desperately needs the teaching and preaching gifts of Jesus, but what else did the Lord do when He was among us? He served. He helped. He comforted. He encouraged. He gave of Himself. And where would we be without these qualities of our Lord among us?

As a pastor-teacher, I've got a high-visibility gift. It may be the most visible of all, because I'm charged to stand in front of God's hungry people and say, "Thus saith the Lord." But how could I do what I do if all of the low-visibility gifts weren't in operation? The fact is, I couldn't—and even that "high-visibility" gift would become invisible. We need the whole church to work together.

It's what the Lord of the church had planned.

Through the gifts of the Spirit, God comes alongside of us to do—in His power—what you and I could never do on our own. So when the world sees and hears the reality of the living Christ as demonstrated through His people living out their gifts, they say, "Whoa, this is different! Let's check this out and see what's happening." And when they come to see what's happening because of the gift, then we can give them Jesus, through the proclamation of God's Word.

Gifts were never given for you to enjoy some privileged relationship with God.

That's what saves them: Receiving the Living Word as revealed in the written Word.

That's what changes you, being controlled by the Spirit of God and understanding His Word.

Some teach today that certain gifts will make you stronger, or closer to God, or elevate you to some higher spiritual plateau. But I just don't see that emphasis in Scripture. Gifts were never given for you to be glorified or for you to enjoy some privileged relationship with God. You already have a privileged relationship! And when we try to use spiritual gifts for that reason, we're on the wrong path. Why? Because that's not the reason they were given.

CYPRUS JOE GETS A NEW NAME

Joseph, a Levite from Cyprus, whom the apostles called
Barnabas (which means Son of Encouragement), sold a
field he owned and brought the money and put it at the
apostles' feet (4:36–37, NIV).

Joseph of Cyprus was already well known to the apostles.

When folks care enough about you to come up with a nickname—especially a *complimentary* nickname that fits your
character—you can bet that you've made some impact in people's
lives.

Everybody loves an encourager.

So it probably wasn't a great shock when Joseph, aka Barnabas, sold off some land and gave all the proceeds to the church.
When he laid that money down at the apostles' feet, you can kind

*Everybody
loves an
encourager.*

of imagine them looking at each other, nod-
ding their heads, and thinking, *That's our boy,
Barnabas. True to form.*

Here was a man who loved to invest himself
in the lives of others. He loved to take his
time, his talents, and his treasure and just pour it out for the good
of the body. That was his inclination, that was his reputation, that
was his spiritual gift. That was what he was known for after the
Holy Spirit took up residence in his life. His nickname, Barnabas,
means "son of consolation" or "son of encouragement."

Do you know what it means to "encourage" someone? It
means to *breathe courage into* that person's soul when he's just
about run out of it. Barnabas, the encourager, was the Spirit's gift
to the body for the common good.

(And by the way, just in case you might have forgotten, so are
you!)

In the Spirit, he was moved to sell off his assets and give them away. And he loved it! Nothing could have made him happier. Now most of us look at his example and say, "Man, that makes me feel kinda bad because our family isn't doing that. Maybe we ought to sell the car and get roller skates."

But listen…God may not have called you to do that. God may not have *gifted* you to do that. The infant church needed and valued that self-giving gift of Barnabas very much. The Holy Spirit had plans for that particular gift that would not only help the church of that day, but would touch the hearts of God's people down through the ages. Barnabas was just being obedient to the Lord by exercising his gift. And do you know what I think? I think on the night after he gave that huge offering, Barnabas went to bed with a smile on his face! He slept like a baby, with no worries. There's nothing that feels better than flowing along with the Holy Spirit when He's blessing people's lives!

To encourage someone means to breathe courage into that person's soul.

So Barnabas became known for his gift and how God was using it to bless and encourage the baby church. It was gifts such as this and a life such as this that led the family of God to change his name: he wasn't going to be plain old Joseph anymore, he was going to be Barnabas, the "son of encouragement."

He was the type of person who would deal with folks that no one else wanted to deal with. His name appears in several places in the book of Acts, and every time it does, you see him acting according to his gift. Why? Because the Holy Spirit had marked his life.

WARNING! DO NOT DUPLICATE

But a certain man named Ananias, with Sapphira, his wife, sold a possession, and kept back part of the price, his wife also knowing of it, and brought a certain part, and laid it at the apostles' feet (5:1–2).

One of the seldom mentioned aspects of the Ananias and Sapphira story is that they were trying to do what you and I often try to do in the body of Christ: We try to imitate the gifts of others instead of allowing the Spirit to fill us and help us exercise our *own* gift.

And the result? No, we may not end up lying dead on the church floor like those two…but we end up missing God's blessing and God's best. And the church misses what we might have contributed if we'd been concentrating on our own gift of the Spirit. Because if He's given Barney over there the gift of giving, He may have given you the gift of helping those who received that financial blessing to administer it, to be better stewards. But if you're trying to be just like Barney, the church will miss *your* gift, and the body will become just a little bit more anemic.

No one's more important than anyone else.

A FRIEND TO THE FRIENDLESS

And when Saul was come to Jerusalem, he tried to join himself to the disciples; but they were all afraid of him, and believed not that he was a disciple. But Barnabas took him, and brought him to the apostles, and declared unto them how he had seen the Lord in the way, and that he had spoken to him, and how he had preached boldly at Damascus in the name of Jesus. And he was with them coming in and going out at Jerusalem (9:26–28).

"But Barnabas…"

Aren't those sweet words? Here was a new Christian feeling like he wanted to crawl under a rock somewhere, but oh my, here comes the son of encouragement. Here comes the Consolation Kid. Every church needs a Barnabas! Every church needs a Barnabas who recognizes his or her gift of encouragement—and then takes it out of the gift wrap!

When Saul (who would one day be Paul) first walked into the church in Jerusalem, the brothers almost had coronaries. They scattered like pheasants flushed out of the brush. These guys were scared to death of him—and with good reason. Wasn't he the same man who'd had believers—both men and women—dragged off to jail and even executed for their faith?

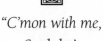

"C'mon with me, Saul, let's go meet the guys."

And now he wanted to be a pal? Now he wanted to drink bad punch and eat cookies at the church fellowships? Hey, these believers were saying, we may be nice, but we're not stupid. And whenever Saul tried to talk to someone, he or she melted into the woodwork, and he was left standing by himself.

But Barnabas...

One of the translations says, "But Barnabas took hold of him...." I like that. Barnabas got an arm around the man's shoulder and said, "C'mon with me, Saul, let's go meet the guys."

Don't those kind of Christians just make you mad? They stretch you right out of your comfort zone. Barnabas was walking around with Saul, introducing him like they were old buddies, and everyone else was wearing sacks over their heads so Saul couldn't identify them! Barnabas was way out ahead of them. Because of his gift, he could almost smell discouragement and uncertainty, and he swooped down on Saul like a hawk and took him by the arm.

But wait a minute...was that acting strange? Or was that just a man acting according to his gifting? There's no way the Consolation Kid was going to stand around when Saul was feeling so lonely and out of place!

He was an encourager. He was the Spirit's gift to the body. (And just another reminder here: *So are you.*)

Nobody wanted to deal with Saul of Tarsus. They could probably all remember aunts and uncles—and maybe even moms and dads and children—this man had had imprisoned or killed. If ever anyone needed to see the gift of encouragement in action, it was Saul. And what brought Barnabas into that picture? It was the gifting of the Spirit. Barnabas probably didn't even have to think twice. No one had to say, "Maybe you oughtta go talk to this guy, Barnabas."

Your gift may lead you into an uncomfortable situation.

You see, when you've got a gift, your gift will lead you to do things that may even surprise *you*. Sometimes that can create an uncomfortable situation. Just look at what happened in Acts 15.

And some days after, Paul [formerly Saul], said unto Barnabas, Let us go again and visit our brethren in every city where we have preached the word of the Lord, and see how they do. And Barnabas determined to take with them John, whose surname was Mark. But Paul thought it not good to take him with them, who departed from them from Pamphylia, and went not with them to the work (15:36–38).

Paul was saying, "Look, the boy quit on us the last missionary journey we were on. I'm not taking him. We can't depend on him, Barnabas! He quit once, he'll quit again."

If anyone should have realized the strength of Barnabas's gift, it should have been Paul! After all, if it hadn't been for Barnabas, Paul might have been a very long time in Jerusalem, cooling his heels while he waited for the church to receive him. So why was he so surprised to see his friend rush to the side of a young man who needed encouragement? Barnabas put his arm around John Mark and said, "Paul, you're giving up on this brother too soon. I see potential."

Paul replied, "I'm glad you do, because I don't. And since you see it, *you* encourage him. I'm going my way and you go yours." So one of the first and most powerful missionary teams the world had ever seen split up. The argument got so sharp that they separated and went on two different missionary journeys.

Though Paul didn't realize it at the time, there would come a day when he would be glad for Barnabas's encouragement of John Mark. Barnabas was simply using his gift in a consistent, persistent manner.

Are you using yours like that? Do you even know what your gift is? If you're not sure, don't waste your time taking some kind of "gifts inventory" test or personality profile. You don't need a counselor to tell you your gift, you need to hear from THE Counselor. What you need to do is get yourself neck-deep in the work of the Lord. After a while, you'll find yourself inclined to do the same sorts of things. You'll find joy in it. You'll find fruit in it. You'll develop a consistent pattern. Other people will see it and note it, and—maybe, over time—even affirm you in it.

Where should you start? How about lending a hand wherever you see a need? Do you have a gift for working with two-year-olds in the church nursery? Maybe not, but those kids still need someone to play with them and change them and teach them. Once you begin moving, getting busy in the work, the Spirit can direct you into a more specific area of service. But if you're not doing anything, just sitting around for lightning to strike, you won't have an opportunity to discover where you fit in.

If you are a Christian, you *do* have a gift of the Holy Spirit for the common good of His people. Are you available to Him to use that gift when a need arises? Are you a willing tool in the hand of the Holy Spirit to minister to God's people?

Let's make it personal. What if Barnabas didn't *feel* like using his gift on certain key occasions? At any one of those crucial moments (and who knows which moments are "crucial" when we're in the middle of them?), what if Barnabas had just decided, "I'm tired today. I need to sleep in a little. I'm not going to be at the service Sunday morning. I'll catch Charles Stanley on the tube."

Where do you start? How about lending a hand wherever you see a need?

So on that morning, that particular characteristic of Jesus Christ doesn't walk through the doors into the worship service. And all those who are discouraged and disheartened and ready to punt the football go home just the way they came—or worse.

- What if Barnabas had said, "Hey, I don't want to sell off my land. It's a great view lot with city sewer. Why should I give it to the church? They probably wouldn't appreciate it anyway. Someone will think I'm just grandstanding and doing this for my own glory." *The church would have lost an example of openhearted generosity that inspired everyone to give of themselves. And Barnabas's name would probably have remained Joe.*

- What if Barnabas had quenched his feelings of compassion for Saul of Tarsus and just walked away from him in Jerusalem? *From a human perspective at least, we wouldn't have most of our New Testament today. The church might have lost its mightiest warrior.*

- What if Barnabas—oh my goodness, praise God this didn't happen—hadn't decided to stick it out with young John Mark, but had just given in and gone with Paul? What if he had said something like this? "I'm with the main man in all the church, I'm with Paul. We're the number-one team; our names will be in lights. I'm going to stuff this gift of mine and go with the flow. Paul, you're right, the sucker quit on us, didn't he? Bye, quitter!" *If he had done that, we wouldn't have had one of the gospels, the book of Mark. And Paul wouldn't have had a strong, faithful helper in his imprisonment, when helpers were few—and not very faithful (see 2 Timothy 4:11).*

The fact is, you don't know who you might have encouraged—or exhorted, or taught, or helped, or directed—just because you thought you had something a little "more important" to do than to be obedient and be in church. And I'm not just talking about your local fellowship…I'm talking about being in THE church. If you're out of town and can't make it to your home fellowship, you can make it to another church where Christ is preached.

Why should I be inconvenienced for using my gift? Because gifts aren't for you.

Your gift in the church, you see, is universal; it's not for one particular church. And if you can't use your gift in every church, maybe you ought to double-check your gift.

Do you know why a lot of us don't want to use our gifts? Because, truthfully, it can sometimes make life inconvenient for us.

THE LONG HAUL WITH PAUL

But Barnabas took him, and brought him to the apostles… and [Saul] was with them coming in and going out at Jerusalem. And he spoke boldly in the name of the Lord Jesus, and disputed against the Grecians; but they went about to slay him, which, when the brethren knew, they brought him down to Caesarea, and sent him forth to Tarsus (9:27, 28–30).

Now, if you're going to yield to the Spirit and use your gift as He directs, it means there will be times when you are seriously inconvenienced.

"Well," you say, "I don't like the sound of that. Why should I be put out for using my gift?"

The answer is simple: because gifts are not for you. We've already established that gifts are for the church, for the common good of God's people. They're not for your benefit, to make you feel good about yourself, or give you some sort of holy glow.

After Barnabas had taken Saul under his wing, things started getting hot for the former Pharisee. So the brothers bought him a one-way ticket to Tarsus and put him on a ship. Then Scripture says that "the churches throughout all Judea, Galilee, and Samaria had peace" (9:31, NKJV). Can't you just hear all the church leaders say, "Whew! I'm glad that guy's out of town for a while. Trouble follows him around like bad cologne."

But do you think that new convert—lonely and frustrated as he might have been—went away alone? I don't think so, either! I think Barnabas packed a couple bags and climbed onto that ship with him. I think that from that time on, until the big split came in Acts 15, Barnabas remained close to Paul. That could have been a period as long as seventeen years.

The fact is, Barnabas's life changed dramatically when he stepped alongside of Saul of Tarsus and said, "I'll stand wit'cha, brother. I'll believe in you. Stick with me." That commitment resulted in Barnabas's leaving his home church, his many friends, and his familiar surroundings. And when the time came for that first missionary journey, the Holy Spirit said, "Separate me Barnabas and Saul for the work unto which I have called them" (13:2).

Life changed for Barnabas the day he obeyed the Spirit and exercised his gift of encouragement with Saul. That gift of his took him into danger and persecution and travels across the known world.

Exercising your gift…might send you across the street—or across the world.

What will exercising your gift do for you?

You never know. It might pull you up out of a rut. It might send you across the street— or across the world. You might find yourself doing things you never dreamed you'd be doing in places you never dreamed you'd be doing them. When I was a rookie with the Dallas Cowboys, do you think I could have ever imagined pastoring a large, multicultural church in Bellevue, Washington? Probably not. But that's where my gift has taken me. And I wouldn't want to be anywhere else on the planet, because being obedient to the Spirit is the only way I want to live.

> Then had the churches rest throughout all Judea and Galilee and Samaria, and were edified; and walking in the fear of the Lord, and in the comfort of the Holy Spirit, were multiplied (9:31).

Most commentaries will tell you that the reason the church rested was because Paul became a believer. He'd been raising so much havoc that when he got saved, the church had some peace and quiet for a while. I can buy that argument for at least 50 percent of the church. But I think the reason the other 50 percent of the church rested was because no one was disturbing the status quo for the fourteen years while he was gone!

If Paul could shake up Jerusalem and make everyone mad at him in those weeks immediately after his salvation, what I want to know is, where was the rest of the church? Why was it so peaceful and easy after Paul headed north? Weren't there any bold believers to step into the gap and bring that city to conviction over their rejection of Jesus?

You and I have the power to shake up people if we're consistently using the gifts and abilities God has given us. We may do it in a highly visible, up-front kind of way, or we may do it behind the scenes, being faithful to exercise our gift and remain obedient to the Spirit—even when the pressure's on.

BRING THAT LADY BACK!

So maybe you find yourself thinking, I probably have a gift of "helps." How could I be that important to the church? Before we finish this chapter, take a minute or so to consider a lady named Tabitha.

> Now in Joppa there was a certain disciple named Tabitha (which translated in Greek is called Dorcas); this woman was abounding with deeds of kindness and charity, which she continually did. And it came about at that time that she fell sick and died; and when they had washed her body, they laid it in an upper room. And since Lydda was near Joppa, the disciples, having heard that Peter was there, sent two men to him, entreating him, "Do not delay to come to us" (9:36–38, NASB).

Tabitha got very sick and died. Now that was a sad thing to happen, but, honestly, people die all the time. But those brothers and sisters in the little town of Joppa just couldn't accept it. Someone in the group remembered that Peter was over in Lydda, a town about twenty miles to the northwest, and they sent their fastest runner to fetch him back to Joppa.

They weren't going after Peter to speak at the memorial service, they wanted Tabitha back from the dead! They loved her and valued her so much they refused to give her up. Even to death!

My question to you and me is this: If you or I died, would people want us back? Would people say, "Oh, he was a good fellow, that Hutcherson. But it's much better that he's not here." As a Christian, are you living your life and exercising your gifts in such a way that you would leave a major gap in the body of Christ if you passed away?

> Then Peter arose and went with them. When he was come, they brought him into the upper chamber; and all the widows stood by him weeping, and showing the coats and garments which Dorcas made, while she was with them. But Peter put them all forth, and kneeled down, and prayed; and turning to the body said, Tabitha, arise. And she opened her eyes; and when she saw Peter, she sat up. And he gave her his hand, and lifted her up; and when he had called the saints and widows, presented her alive (9:39–41).

Peter walked into that upper room where the body was lying, and he found himself surrounded by widows, crying and pushing things under his nose for him to see. "Oh, Peter," someone said to him, "you've just got to bring her back! Last winter I didn't know how in the world I was going to make it—didn't even have a coat! And in walks Tabitha with a coat she made herself!"

And someone else said, "Oh, Peter. She just can't leave us like this! I remember last year when I had my baby—and you know when you have a baby you don't like anybody, especially your husband! And it was amazing to me; I was sitting there crying, at my wit's end, and in walks Tabitha. She had problems all her own, but man, she took me on. She took the baby away for several hours and said, 'Girl, have some rest.' And not only did she do that, but she made a casserole for dinner and handed me this pretty baby blanket."

"Oh, Peter, you've got to bring her back. She was always taking food to the poor and to the old folks."

"Oh, Peter, we just can't get along without this lady!"

Tabitha had the gift of helping, one of the characteristics of Jesus Christ. And her gift was so important to the church that when she died, she left a hole that you could drive a truck through.

Would you and I leave that kind of hole? Would you and I be missed like that, because of our touch on the lives of others? Let me tell you something straightforward, friend. Many of us *wouldn't* be missed because we're so caught up in ourselves and in our businesses and in our families that we don't have time for anyone else.

But once we begin to exercise our gifts in obedience to God, the Holy Spirit won't let us get away with that anymore.

Let's start today...and see where He leads us!

BECAUSE
WE'RE AFRAID
OF
PERSECUTION

There's one thing I've noticed about affliction.

It tends to get your whole attention.

Blessings can fly across the horizons of our lives like flocks of geese heading south, and we look up and say, "Oh yeah, isn't that nice?" But if you take a hammer and hit your thumb, suddenly every aspect of your body gets involved in that pain! Nothing gets your full and complete attention like affliction.

And there's nothing like Christians suffering together or facing danger together to knit the hearts of those believers and make them one.

I became a Christian in my senior year of high school. And if I'd thought life was tough before…things *really* heated up after that. The blacks at school turned against me because I had to give up my hate for whites. They thought I was "selling out" and wouldn't have anything more to do with me. The whites still hated me because of my old reputation. There were already threats on my life from the Ku Klux Klan. It wasn't even safe for me to walk to school. I had never been more isolated in my life.

So can you imagine? A senior in high school with no friends at all, no one to talk to. Hated and ridiculed by the blacks, hated and threatened by the whites. (I guess that's what you'd call "equal opportunity.") So I was stuck by myself. Talk about lonely! There was no one to turn to but the Lord.

I used to come to Him day after day, night after night, with my hurts and my pain and my loneliness. It was just me and God, and I grew more than I could have ever believed possible.

But oh man, the aloneness! The desertion and fear that I felt in those days! But my Lord knew all about it. He sent two white Campus Crusade guys along to love me and be my friends. They told me, "Hey Hutch, we'll pick you up after school every day. We'll drop you off at home. We'll pick you up in the morning and take you to school. We'll be there, man."

Come to find out these two young men had been praying for me for almost three years. They would come to the stands and watch football practice, and the Lord put me on their hearts. At first they didn't even know my name. They just prayed for the number on my football jersey. They prayed for me when I was a renegade…when I was hateful…when I was out to hurt and injure as many white guys as I possibly could. They used to say to each other, "If this guy could get turned around for the Lord—just imagine what would happen!"

Affliction tends to get your whole attention.

Then, after I accepted Christ, and during my isolation in that senior year, they took the risk to come alongside me and be my friends. That was God's provision to get me through my senior year. And we've remained friends to this very day.

One of the things I've noticed through the years is that when God wants you to move in a certain direction, when He really wants to command your attention, He has no problem at all doing that. He might use a still, small voice, or He might use a two-by-four alongside your head, but He knows very well how to stir things up in your life; He knows how to eliminate petty distractions *fast*.

Let me illustrate. In our bathroom at home, there are several bottles of perfume. Ladies have perfume, men have cologne—*eau de toilette*, which means "good-smellin' in the bathroom."

But I've noticed something about that perfume and cologne. The liquid fragrance contained in those bottles will stay there; it will be perfectly satisfied just hanging out on the bottom of the bottle if there isn't some kind of outside influence that comes around to shake things up. It will sit there for *years* and won't even move unless something touches it, shakes it, tips it, or sprays it. Without an outside influence, that perfume will sit in there until doomsday. All that nice fragrance and sweet-smelling stuff will remain bottled up, and it won't do anybody a bit of good.

As I've thought about it, that seems like a pretty fair picture of the Christian life. If God doesn't allow an outside influence to come into our lives from time to time—a little pressure, a little bumping around, a little shaking—we'll just sit on our bottoms and won't even move. We'll keep our testimony bottled up tight. God has to add a little bit of agitation sometimes before the perfume of the Lord Jesus gets out of the bottle and makes a difference in the world.

It was no different in the book of Acts....

GIVING THE AUTHORITIES GRIEF

And as they spoke unto the people, the priests, and the captain of the temple, and the Sadducees, came upon them, being grieved that they taught the people, and preached through Jesus the resurrection from the dead. And they laid hands on them, and put them in custody unto the next day; for it was now eventide (4:1–3).

Peter and John had just performed an astonishing miracle, healing a man born lame who had sat for years at the Beautiful Gate of the temple. Now why do you think the priests, the captain of the temple, and the Sadducees "came upon" these disciples and "laid hands on them"? Why were these men in authority so *grieved*, as the Scripture says?

Back in Jesus' day (just as today), there were two groups within the religious community.

Liberals and conservatives.

Now, when it comes to labels like that, I just call myself a Christian who believes in the Bible. But folks who like to pigeon-hole other folks sometimes call me a fundamental conservative member of the religious right...with maybe a *touch* of sensitivity.

The liberals and conservatives of that day were battling over issues just as they battle today. When Jesus walked on the earth, the religious liberals ran the show. (There's always somebody "in control," however shaky and temporary that control may be.) The name of that liberal party was the Sadducees. As with liberals the world over, they had major problems with Scripture, their main problem being that they didn't *believe* it. That started them off on the wrong foot before they ever walked through the door.

The Sadducees didn't believe in resurrection or life after death. When you died, as far as they were concerned it was *over*, Jack; you were annihilated. They didn't believe in angels or spirits, either. As a matter of fact, there wasn't very much that they did believe, other than holding on to power right here on earth. You might call them the humanists of their day; their focus was on this world alone. Now the conservatives of that era, the Pharisees party, did believe in angels, spirits, and the immortality of the soul.

These two groups were, however, completely united on one front. On one issue of the day, the liberals and conservatives were in perfect harmony. Neither party had any time for Jesus. They could agree on that.

So when Jesus walked on the earth for those three and a half years of intensive ministry, both groups took shots at him. The liberals, since they were top dogs, came after Him first. They launched their brightest and sharpest arrows at Him in public and came back busted, busted, busted. The conservatives had their chance, too, and didn't fare much better. All of their best arguments and verbal traps, sprung by their smoothest spokesmen and buttoned-down lawyers, came up flat empty. They might as well have been firing blanks.

So what did they do? They got together, conservatives and liberals, had a summit meeting, and came together on a plan. If they couldn't shut Him up, they'd just kill Him, and then their problems would be over. Right? With that troublesome teacher from Nazareth safely six feet under, they could go back to doing what they did best: fighting with each other.

But then came the Resurrection.

And then came Pentecost.

And then came a ragtag group of disciples doing amazing miracles that couldn't be denied, and talking all over town in the name of *Jesus*. So the rulers hadn't put the lid on this "Jesus sect" after all. As a matter of fact, the lid was blowing off higher than ever.

Do you see why they were grieved? Do you see why the Sadducees said, "Go arrest those boys!"?

Being grieved that they taught the people, and preached through Jesus the resurrection from the dead (4:2).

Number one, they didn't believe in Jesus, and number two, they didn't believe in the Resurrection; and here were two former fishermen who had the nerve to heal a man lame from birth right on the steps of the temple. And to make matters worse, they did it in front of a big crowd, and then gave the glory to this Jesus who just wouldn't go away! This was just too much.

Let me tell you what's really nasty. Anytime you have a liberal religious group, you always have someone trying to figure a way to work with the government. And that's what was going on here. The Sadducees had the power, and they were allowed by the Romans to keep that power and prestige just as long as they kept the people under control. But the Sadducees knew that if this Jesus movement started rolling, Rome might get a little excited about claims of some new Jewish king in town. They'd march in, flex their muscle, and the Sadducees would go from the penthouse to the outhouse overnight.

They were more than just a tad upset, they were torn in their deepest roots.

So what did they have to do? They had to stamp out this Jesus talk *fast*.

Now you begin to really catch on as to why these guys were popping Tums when they heard about the miracle and the big crowd at the temple gate. What could they do? There was the healed man standing there in front of everyone saying, "That's right, I'm the same guy! You passed by me every day when I was begging outside the gate. Check me out now; am I cool or what? Bring me shoes, I can use 'em now!" This guy was just letting it roll out.

And the Sadducees were *grieved*.

This isn't a light word Dr. Luke used here. They were more than just a tad upset, they were torn in their deepest roots about what was going on.

"I thought we got rid of that guy Jesus! I thought we wasted Him. Didn't we see Him die on the cross? Now here we are again with the crowds and the rumors and that Man's name being whispered all over town! We're getting nowhere!"

And they laid hands on them....

That's a real nice way of saying they dissed the disciples! They locked up the boys and wanted to throw away the key. But they couldn't do it because they had to have a trial.

...and put them in custody unto the next day; for it was now eventide (4:3).

Now if Peter and John went up to the temple at the ninth hour, 3:00 P.M., by the time they healed the guy, preached a sermon, and had their little encounter with the Jerusalem PD, it was after 6:00 P.M.

After they laid hands on them and threw them in the slammer, these authorities must have said to each other, "We're not going to do night court. No, we'll let 'em cool their heels overnight in jail and see how sassy they are in the morning."

That was the strategy, and you can imagine how it might have worked. Have you ever received a call from an acquaintance or friend who said, "I'd like to get together and talk to you about something. How about tomorrow?"

When the church is persecuted for the name of Jesus, we are strengthened.

What do you do until you meet with that person? What do you do while you're waiting? Your mind is working overtime, isn't it? You're thinking, I wonder what in the world they want to talk about—and why couldn't they just tell me on the phone? What have I done now? What have I said? You get a funny, queasy sort of feeling in your stomach waiting for that kind of "appointment."

"We're going to let them think about it all night," these authorities were saying. "We're going to let them fret. By the time tomorrow rolls around, they'll be so scared they'll think we're going to kill them."

That's probably the way their reasoning went, and it's a common misconception down to this day. We tend to think that if the church is persecuted, if the authorities muscle us and try to shut Christians up and shut the church down, that we're going to lose strength.

As a matter of fact, the Bible teaches just the opposite. Scripture shows us that when the church is persecuted for the name of Jesus, we are strengthened. And instead of losing strength, we lose fear. Here's what I mean: There's only one way to lose fear, and that is to be put in fearful situations and discover firsthand that God is fully able to care for you.

- All of us want the comfort of God...but none of us want to be in an uncomfortable situation to find out how great that comfort can be.

- All of us want God to come through for us...but none of us want to be put in a position where He's our only hope of rescue.

- All of us want the peace of God in our lives...but none of us want our own peace removed to make room for God's peace.

- All of us want the provision of God...but none of us want to run out of our own provision so that we might truly experience His.

The truth is, you and I *grow* under persecution for Jesus Christ—and so does His church. Let me prove it to you. Check out what happened after Peter and John had been seized and escorted away by the authorities:

But many of them who heard the word believed; and the number of the men was about five thousand (4:4).

PREACHING IN THE POWERHOUSE

And it came to pass, on the next day, that their rulers, and elders, and scribes, and Annas, the high priest, and Caiaphas, and John, and Alexander, and as many as were of the kindred of the high priest, were gathered together at Jerusalem (4:5–6).

They brought them to the Sanhedrin. The powerhouse.

For a Jew of that day, there was no more intimidating, high-pressure place to land. This was Congress, the Supreme Court, the Oval Office, an IRS audit, and traffic court all rolled into one, and you'd better believe those officials on the Sanhedrin were counting on that intimidation.

Now when you and I get persecuted or under pressure, we start crying, complaining, and getting uptight. Not John and Peter. For them, this was the Super Bowl. Unless I miss my bet, when they felt this very first pinch of persecution they partied all night! Can't you just imagine them high-fiving in the cell? "Gimme five, man, we're going to give it to them tomorrow. We're going to be in front of the *Sanhedrin!* We've got the most important people in all of Jerusalem gathered in one place. Can you believe it? And they're going to have to listen to us tomorrow. They don't want to hear the name of Jesus, so let's be sure to lay it on 'em early and often!"

If God allows you to be persecuted, it's because He has a purpose in it all.

Do you know one of the reasons why God allows you to be persecuted and pressured? Because you've got something to say that the men and women putting you under pressure need to hear. It's an opportunity to bring the gospel before people who might otherwise never hear it. But what do we usually do? We try to bail out. We cry, "Why me? Lord, get me out of this QUICK!"

The truth is, we need to be ready both to encounter and endure persecution. If our sovereign God allows you to be persecuted, it's because He's got a purpose in it all. And since He's let you be a part of that purpose, you can count on the fact that no one else can fulfill that purpose in the way that you can.

Check this out. After Peter and John had finished testifying, those graybeards on the Sanhedrin were blown away. Why? Here's what the Word says:

> Now when they saw the boldness of Peter and John, and
> perceived that they were uneducated and untrained men,
> they marveled. And they realized that they had been with
> Jesus (4:13, NKJV).

Do you see? Is that smokin'? It was because Peter and John were who they were—uncultured, uneducated, blue-collar working guys—that their message came through with such power. No one else could have delivered that message as effectively as they were able to do in that moment. The most educated lawyer or brilliant orator couldn't have made the impact that these two fishermen with dirt under their fingernails were able to make. That's why God put them there!

Does that get you fired up? Aren't you glad you bought this book? If this stuff doesn't get you excited, I don't know what to do, because I can't get excited for you!

There was one more reason why Peter was so primed for this group that was supposed to intimidate him. This was the very same bunch that gave Jesus over to be crucified. The last time he'd faced a pressure situation like this, while Jesus was on trial for His life, Peter had crumbled like a stale cookie. Now he had a chance to declare his Lord's name before the very people who had arrested Him.

Here's something we can learn from this: If God gives you an opportunity to stand up for Him and you fail the first time, He's going to put you back in it. So be prayed up, filled up with the Spirit, and stay ready!

Peter had said, "Oh goodness, Lord, You don't have to worry about *me*. I'm a man's man. I've got hair on my chest. I'll fight for You. I'll follow You to the death." Jesus replied, "Peter, you're going to deny Me before the cock crows three times."

Now the Lord has Peter and John in front of the Sanhedrin, Annas the high priest, and Caiaphas, the man who really wielded the power. It was Caiaphas who had been high priest when they crucified Christ. And when Peter looks up, there's that sour old boy glaring down at him from his lofty cushioned seat.

Do people around you take note that you've been with Jesus?

Peter gets even more excited. Why? Because he realizes God is giving him a second chance. The name "Caiaphas" actually means "cock crows." Isn't that great? It's as though the Lord is saying to Peter, "I put you in front of them before, Peter, and you denied Me. Will you deny Me this time in front of the Cock Crow?"

And Peter says, "Not this time, Lord. I've got Your Holy Spirit in me!"

Let me ask you a question. Are you allowing the Holy Spirit to make that kind of difference in your life? Are you allowing Him to fill you with boldness, patience, endurance, and a desire to follow Christ that just grips your heart? Do people around you take note that you have been with Jesus (4:13)?

And when they had set them in the midst, they asked, By what power, or by what name, have ye done this? (4:7)

What a question! If the Sanhedrin had only known—you don't ask Spirit-filled believers a question like that unless you want an earful! Peter and John had probably been praying, "Lord, please give us an opening, just a little crack in the door so that we can tell them where we stand." And then, hardly before folks got settled in their seats for the big show, the first question they're asked is: "By what power and by what name are you out there preaching and healing?"

Whoa! Swing open the door! Roll out the red carpet! Step up to the mike! What an opportunity. Can you imagine them looking at each other saying, "Who's going to talk first? Me, me, me!"

When the door opened, these men didn't hesitate. They didn't try to ingratiate themselves with these powerful men, and they didn't waste time on flattery or idle chitchat. They boldly declared the name of Jesus, and the Sanhedrin (for once) were speechless. They had nothing to say.

Filled with the Holy Spirit, we need to prepare ourselves to do the very same thing.

WHAT PERSECUTION DOES

And being let go, they went to their own company, and reported all that the chief priests and elders had said unto them. And when they heard that, they lifted up their voice to God with one accord... (4:23–24).

Back out on the streets, Peter and John called the church together and gave a report of their meeting before the Sanhedrin and all the threats and warnings that had been uttered by the authorities. And how did the church respond? They turned to the Lord with one accord. They went to the throne of God together, side by side, shoulder to shoulder. And when they were finished praying, "the place was shaken where they were assembled together" (4:31).

That's some powerful praying! And look where it all started: Persecution.

Persecution drove them together

It was persecution that brought the church together.

It was persecution that dropped them to their knees together.

It was persecution that led them to pray for even more boldness in the face of serious official threats.

Persecution drives true believers together and weeds out those who are only along for a joy ride. It creates a tender, generous, giving church (see Acts 4:34–35). Now, none of us want persecution, but at the same time, we want that kind of church! So why should we whine and cry and try to run from persecution when God is gracious enough to send it our way?

It was persecution that led them to pray for even more boldness.

You may be saying, "Wait a minute, Hutch, aren't you getting a little narrow-minded here? Isn't there some other way that we can experience oneness and boldness and room-shaking prayer without persecution?"

Sure there is. But God knows us! He knows that, for many of us, this is the only way that we're going to experience these deeper experiences of the Christian life.

Persecution drove them to worship

They lifted up their voice to God with one accord, and said, Lord, thou art God, who hast made heaven, and earth, and the sea, and all that in them is… (4:24).

That's praise and worship! Nobody was complaining about the worship in *that* service. No one was uptight about the children's program. No one was checking his watch. No one was griping about the organ or piano or guitars or song selection in *that* church meeting. Persecution melted away all the distractions and peripheral arguments. Those folks knew they had to lay hold of God, and they found comfort in doing it together.

Persecution drove them into the Word

These believers were *excited* about this clash with the ruling authorities. Why were they so excited? Were they masochists? Were they nuts? They'd been jailed and they'd been threatened; they knew very well they could be killed, just as Jesus had been killed. Why were they so pumped?

Because they were seeing Scripture fulfilled before their very eyes! The thrill of that experience overrode the threats and persecutions. The happiness of seeing the Word of God fulfilled in their midst made them forget all about not being comfortable.

> …Who, by the mouth of thy servant, David, hast said, Why did the nations rage, and the peoples imagine vain things? The kings of the earth stood up, and the rulers were gathered together against the Lord, and against his Christ (4:25–26).

Check that out. These believers looked at their circumstances, looked at the threats, then looked at God's Word and said, "Yes! God is doing exactly what He said He was going to do. Here are the rulers taking their stand against God's anointed. So we can be excited even though it's uncomfortable for us!"

What did they do? They went straight to the Word. They quoted Psalm 2 to give them perspective on what was happening to them. They looked at their circumstances, saw that those circumstances were fulfilling the Word, and they forgot their discomfort and rejoiced.

Sometimes you and I find ourselves complaining rather than rejoicing when we're under pressure from nonbelievers. That's because we don't know the Word. We don't understand that God is simply doing what He said He was going to do. What does the Word say?

> Yes, and all who desire to live godly in Christ Jesus will suffer persecution (2 Timothy 3:12, NKJV).
> Blessed are you when men hate you, and when they exclude you, and revile you, and cast out your name as evil, for the Son of Man's sake (Luke 6:22, NKJV).

We complain because we don't know the Word. Can you imagine that group of believers in Acts 4 screaming and crying, "Oh God, I can't believe it. Here we are standing up for You, and these people out here are just blasting us! When are You going to come and protect us?"

No, they'd read the Word, and they knew from Psalm 2 that although all the kings and earthly powers would deny Jesus and reject His authority, it was only a temporary situation! In the end, they would be on the winning team. Kings and queens and Sanhedrins and Caesars could come and go, but God had said, "Yet I have set My King on My holy hill of Zion" (Psalm 2:6, NKJV).

Sometimes I believe that God doesn't come along and deliver us from our pressure situations because we've neglected or been disobedient to His Word. If we would read and devour the Word, we'd be rejoicing in those times of pressure and persecution, because we'd realize He was doing just what His Word said He would do.

And now, Lord, behold their threatenings; and grant unto thy servants, that with all boldness they may speak thy word (4:29).

"Lord," they were saying, "we don't want out of this situation You've placed us in. We just don't want to be intimidated or feel squashed by the whole thing. Help us to be bold to speak for You and to take our stand."

Did God appreciate a prayer like that? Check this out.

And when they had prayed, the place was shaken where they were assembled together; and they were all filled with the Holy Spirit, and they spoke the word of God with boldness. And the multitude of those that believed were of one heart and of one soul (4:31–32).

They had the kind of church everyone wants. And they were willing to pay the price. Now, God doesn't usually ask you and me today to put our lives on the line as those believers were doing (At least not yet!). What God asks us today is to put our *reputations* on the line, and you and I are not man enough or woman enough to do even that.

If we were, maybe we'd see some shakin' going on where *we* go to church.

GOD TIPS THE PERFUME BOTTLE

And at that time there was a great persecution against the church which was at Jerusalem; and they were all scattered abroad throughout the regions of Judea and Samaria.... Therefore, they that were scattered abroad went everywhere preaching the word (8:1, 4).

After the death of Stephen, the first martyr, the sky fell in on believers living in the environs of Jerusalem. Although they had seen persecution before, they'd never seen anything like this. Men, women, and children had to leave their homes and flee Jerusalem for their lives.

It's one thing to go out, as they went out, but it's another thing to go out with a purpose. When these believers were scattered, they didn't start screaming how unfair it all was. They didn't go out with an attitude. "Here I am walking with God and now I'm being persecuted and, boy, if talking about Jesus is going to bring persecution, I'm just going to keep my mouth shut!"

He's still in the business of tipping over perfume bottles.

How many of us have said this one before: "I tried it God's way, but it got me in trouble!"? You didn't hear the believers in Acts 8 crying about that. They went out, spreading the gospel as they went.

The church didn't do what God had called it to do, so God allowed some pressure, some persecution, and some suffering to spread the church out. It took the heat and intensity of this concentrated attack to compel the church to do what the Lord of the church had already called her to do:

> But ye shall receive power, after the Holy Spirit is come upon you; and ye shall be witnesses unto me both in Jerusalem, and in all Judea, and in Samaria, and unto the uttermost part of the earth (1:8).

They'd gotten the "Jerusalem" part of that command, all right, but then they'd been content to settle down. God needed to come in and tip that perfume bottle so that the fragrance of Christ might spread into Samaria (Philip started that ball rolling), Asia Minor, Europe, and even Africa.

He's still in the business of tipping perfume bottles. He's still in the business of moving His kids out of their comfort zones. Why? Because Christians still tend to content themselves with huddling together behind the safety of four walls with stained-glass windows. And this world of ours has never needed the fragrance of Jesus more than it needs it now.

Are you willing to be shaken up a little? Are you willing to be tipped?

STEPHEN ON MY MIND

When Saul of Tarsus finally became a believer in Acts 9, you might say that it took a bolt of lightning to get his attention.

But I think the Lord *already* had the attention of the man who would come to be known as Paul the apostle. Paul had seen, heard, and been involved with every believer he chased down, apprehended, and threw in jail. And there was one thing this persecutor of the church saw again and again. What was it? The witness of believers under persecution, who refused to deny their allegiance to the Lord Jesus Christ.

He heard every word of Stephen, the whole sermon. And after Stephen had been fatally stoned by the mob, Paul was standing right there to hear the young man's last words: "Behold, I see the heavens opened, and the Son of man standing on the right hand of God.... Lord, lay not this sin to their charge" (7:56, 60).

God needed a witness to die right at the feet of Paul. He needed that perfume of Christ to be poured out right in front of him. And perhaps the greatest sacrifice Stephen made was in being a good witness even when his life was being taken from him. *"Lord, lay not this sin to their charge."*

Those words must have echoed in Paul's brain every day of his life. And not only Stephen's words. Paul had been aware that every Christian he threw in jail had only to renounce Jesus and he would be set free. But again and again, those Christian men and women facing imprisonment and death said, "My life is not worth anything if I deny my Lord and Savior."

Paul heard it over and over and over and over again. He smelled that fragrance of Jesus time after time in places and situations that shouldn't have been fragrant at all. So when Jesus appeared to him on the road to Damascus, he must have said to himself, "I may be blinded by this light, but I smell something familiar!"

My question to you and me is simply this: Do we stand strong in the midst of those who antagonize us? Do people see us standing courageously and responding graciously as believers when things don't go our way? Are our godly responses playing over and over in the minds of unbelievers? Can they smell the fragrance of Jesus?

Better to be tipped a little—or even broken—than to collect dust on some shelf.

BECAUSE WE'RE BOGGED DOWN BY MURMURING

And in those days, when the number of the disciples was multiplied, there arose a murmuring of the Grecians against the
Hebrews, because their widows were neglected in the daily min-
istration. Then the twelve called the multitude of the disciples
unto them, and said, It is not fitting that we should leave the
word of God, and serve tables. Wherefore, brethren, look among
you for seven men of honest report, full of the Holy Spirit and
wisdom, whom we may appoint over this business (6:1–3).

As we study the book of Acts, I don't think it would be very
difficult to establish that every attack recorded against the
church could also be used as an attack against you or your
family as you try to follow God's path for your life. You see, Satan isn't
all that original in his tactics. He just keeps dragging out the same old
traps and the same old techniques he's used against believers for centuries.

Why should he change? They still work! He just keeps them oiled
and maintained for each new generation of Christians coming along.

As we've seen in the book of Acts, the first means he may use
against believers is external opposition or pressure...something outside
of your control. These are circumstances and events that slam into your
life and try to knock you off your foundation. It's like a mudslide that
threatens to pull your life and your home down around your ears.

Sometimes that's all it takes. Believers who haven't built their lives on the Word of God can be flattened—washed away—like the foolish man Jesus spoke of in Matthew 7:26–27. If you build your house on the sand, watch out for that first storm, Jack, because it'll be all over.

When that doesn't work, however, when the believer allows those circumstances to push him toward the Lord Jesus rather than away from Him, the enemy has to try something different. If outside pressure doesn't work, he's going to try an *inside* attack.

SATAN'S "STUNTS"

The words "inside attack" and "outside attack" make me think back to my football days. The whole game of football is based upon "How can we penetrate the other team's defense?" or "How can we penetrate the other team's offense and throw it off?"

On the defensive side, we had plays called "stunts." We would try to send in more people than the offensive line could block at one time. (Have you ever seen a linebacker slip through the line untouched and deck a quarterback who doesn't even see him coming? It's a beautiful sight.)

If you build your house on the sand, watch out for that first storm, Jack!

Now, in our defensive schemes, we'd usually go with an inside attack first, our line surging ahead trying to break through and disrupt what the other team wanted to do. If that didn't rock 'em, we'd send a linebacker or two sprinting through the middle. We'd do this especially in passing situations, where the offense was trying to move quickly down the field and chew up big chunks of yardage.

It's the same thing in our spiritual lives. Whenever we try to do something big for Christ and we're making real gains, the enemy will try to "stunt" us. He'll try to throw us off. He'll hit with extra pressure from the inside, if he can. If we block it, he'll switch strategies and come at us from the outside.

That's the whole football analogy. If I can attack your defense and push holes up the middle, I'm going to run up the middle all day long. And if Satan can get us from the inside—if he can constantly set us back on our heels—why should he try the outside? He won't change unless that strategy stops working. And he will never stop attacking.

Satan says, "If I can't get ya from the outside, I'll go to the inside."

That's one thing about football. You play to *win*. So if the inside isn't working, you go to the outside. If that doesn't work, you mix it up. But you never give up!

Satan says, "If I can't get ya from the outside, I'll go to the inside. And if I can't get you from the inside, I'll go after the outside—and maybe I'll catch you when you're not ready one of these times, and I'll lay you flat."

When the enemy goes inside, he centers his attack on something inside your home, inside your church, inside your life. You can rest assured that when one strategy fails, the other one isn't far behind.

The key is that you and I remember to keep God's perspective in these things (and how can we do that unless we're saturating our lives and our minds with the Word of God?). When we lose that eternal perspective, we'll find ourselves saying, "Why is it that every time something *good* happens in my life, something *bad* seems to follow?"

Have you ever said or thought something like that? You've got the wrong perspective! God knows it takes those "bad things" to mold us, and He knows very well that those negative pressures are on their way—plenty of them. So what does He do? Being the kind of Father He is, He throws in a little good with the bad, so that bad won't seem quite so bad! But instead of being grateful for those moments of sunshine, we get frustrated, we get upset, and we get down.

Throughout the whole Old Testament, God used the Law to drive men to a Savior (Romans 7:7–8). In the New Testament God uses life itself to drive you to Jesus. His whole mission in our lives, according to Romans 8:28–29, is to conform us to the image of His Son. Yet when we encounter circumstances intended to do just that, what do we do?

We complain and murmur.

We lose our perspective.

Just remember...when great things are happening in the church and in your life and in your family, opposition and satanic attack aren't far behind! Look again at verse 1 of Acts 6:

> And in those days, when the number of the disciples was multiplied...

Those were great days. The opposition of the authorities hadn't stopped them! They'd been threatened. They'd been hauled into court. They'd been thrown in jail. They'd been tortured and beaten. And what was the result? "The number of disciples was multiplied"!

But right in the midst of these Christians making a tremendous impact in society—people being saved, disciples growing in their faith, the assemblies of believers bulging and spreading—the church is faced with its first serious case of murmuring.

Has that happened in your home? Has that happened in your church? Has that happened in your heart? Why in the world are we so surprised?

THE INSIDE ATTACK

Some of the disciples began murmuring because one group of widows seemed to be favored over another group of widows in the daily distribution of food. In verse 1, we read that one group was "Grecian" (or Hellenist) and another group was "Hebrew."

Hellenists were Jews that spoke in Greek, and the Hebrews were the local Jews that spoke in Hebrew. A Hellenistic Jew was any Jew that wasn't from Palestine. They had been brought up in the Greek language, the dominant language of the day, but remained Jewish in their beliefs. When the gospel was preached, both groups embraced Jesus and ended up in the church in Jerusalem.

Here was a little cross-cultural action going on! It was a test for the young church. If they couldn't handle two groups of *Jews* getting along, how were they going to handle it when Samaritans and Gentiles showed up on the doorstep? Hmmm?

There was lots of money flowing into the church at that time, "for as many as were possessors of lands or houses sold them, and brought the prices of the things that were sold, and laid them down at the apostles' feet; and distribution was made unto every man according as he had need" (4:34–35). This was supposed to be an equitable distribution; everyone was equal. But as we all know, there's always the perception that some are more equal than others!

At least that's what one group in the church thought. And they began to murmur. There's some "muttering" under the breath implied in that word; some private grumbling that started to spread unhappiness and dissension—like poison gas seeping up through the sewer.

We've seen it a thousand times before, haven't we? Right in the middle of blessing and joy and good things happening, somebody on the inside gets their feelings hurt or feels slighted somehow and begins to murmur. And when that happens, it's like a cloud passing in front of the sun. One minute you're warm and then—suddenly you feel a chill. Suddenly it doesn't feel so warm anymore.

On one of the football teams I played for, we had a coach who was a master of the put-down. I remember an incident about halfway through one season, when things were falling apart for us and we weren't having the success that we wanted. The coach walked into the locker room one day, looked around, and said, "I just want you guys to know something. I will tolerate you until I can replace you."

All the guys kind of looked around at each other as if to say,

"Thanks, Coach. This really inspires us to want to play." He may have *thought* he was motivating us, but all he succeeded in doing was killing the little bit of motivation we still had. He made us feel hopeless!

But that's what murmuring does, doesn't it? It kills hope. It kills joy. It kills motivation.

It happens in marriage, doesn't it? A wife will break her neck getting a great dinner on the table (maybe after working all day herself), and the husband will pick out one piddly thing to complain about. What does that do to the atmosphere at the table? It poisons it, doesn't it? It casts a big shadow over the light and joy that could have been shared that night.

Right in the middle of blessing and joy... someone feels slighted and begins to murmur.

Or how about a husband who's been working on some of his old bad habits and making good progress, too. For a whole week he's picked up his dirty socks, carried his own dirty dishes to the sink, and done more than grunt when his wife has spoken to him. But then she nails him for something really trivial, and he says to himself, *Hey, what's the use? There's no use tryin', 'cause this boy's never going to measure up.*

We have a tendency to ignore the hundred good things and focus all our attention on the two or three things that really bug us...and it poisons our relationships.

It's the same in a church. Even when the Word of God is being faithfully preached week after week, and people are coming to the Lord and growing like crazy, folks will find the two or three things the leadership hasn't got to yet and they'll begin to mutter and murmur and spread their poison.

That's why the Lord gave us the Instruction Manual for the church. And here in the book of Acts, we can see how the leadership handled this situation.

GET THE LEADERSHIP INVOLVED

Then the twelve called the multitude of the disciples unto them, and said, It is not fitting that we should leave the word of God, and serve tables (6:2).

There's no way of telling how much time passed between verse 1 and verse 2—between the time when the murmuring began and when the leaders weighed in. It could have been fast. On the other hand, it could have been a situation like the one that happens so often in churches today: the leadership hears about it after the complaint has made the rounds through half the congregation!

However long it took, the leaders responded right away after the matter came to their attention. Boom!—there was a meeting. And it wasn't just a group of elders meeting behind closed doors, either; the whole church was summoned. That's how seriously the leaders took this matter of murmuring.

Sometimes we don't give the leaders a chance—we'd rather whisper and grumble.

Now what if those leaders hadn't responded so quickly? The poison would have kept spreading, wouldn't it? And Satan would have won a victory.

But sometimes we don't even want to give the leaders a chance. We'd rather whisper and mutter and grumble than get the leaders involved. After all, if they got involved, they might actually solve the problem—and then there wouldn't be anything to grumble about. Instead of seeking to get the problem attended to, some of us would rather find others to murmur with us. We'd rather say, "Yeah, things look good on the *surface,* but I know a lot of people who'd tell you that things aren't so cool." And just like that, we begin to cast a shadow over what the Lord is accomplishing in our midst. We think that murmuring is the next gift of the Holy Spirit! Or worse, we'll say we have the gift of "exhortation," and use that as a license to go around dumping our negative garbage on people whenever we feel like it.

In this instance, it was a problem between the Greek-speakers and the Hebrew-speakers. But what if it was today, and black people were feeling they weren't being treated fairly in the church? What if there were some Filipinos in the fellowship, and they didn't feel like they were getting equal attention and care? How would we handle that today?

I don't think the church today would do what they did in Acts 6. What we would do is call for a multicultural task force or committee to come together. We'd have sensitivity classes. We'd get so involved with being sensitive to everyone and their backgrounds that we would never get the problem solved. The "sensitivity committee" would become a permanent fixture. We might never get anywhere with the issue, but boy, would we be sensitive!

The way to attack a spiritual problem is with spiritual people.

But what did the apostles do? They told this big, all-church meeting, "It is not fitting that we should leave the word of God, and serve tables."

Wow! What if church leadership said that today? Could we handle that? What if the church had a group of ladies who were feeling neglected? What if there was an all-church meeting and I as the pastor stood up and said, "Yes, I recognize there's a problem here, and we need to deal with it. But your problem isn't as important as the Word of God. We cannot allow this problem to pull away our focus from the ministry of the Word."

What kind of reaction would I get? "Reaction" would be the right word. We would have some serious reaction going on. Chain reaction! Nuclear reaction! Now, I didn't say that addressing people's concerns wasn't important. I said the problem isn't as important as making sure I'm focused on the preaching and teaching of God's Word.

The apostles had no fear to say, "This is an issue, but it *must not* distract us from the main ministry here. No issue is that important!" Today, however, people hop from one church to another—not because of important doctrinal issues, but because their feelings have been hurt. Their needs haven't been addressed as quickly as they think they should have been addressed. And they begin to murmur.

Attack Spiritual Problems with Spiritual People

What did the apostles say?

> Wherefore, brethren, look among you for seven men of honest report, full of the Holy Spirit and wisdom, whom we may appoint over this business (6:3).

I love this. If we've got murmuring going on in the church, we've got a spiritual problem. And the way to attack a spiritual problem is with spiritual people!

The first thing the church needs to do is find some godly men to put in positions of leadership. (And when I speak of men in "leadership," I mean pastors and elders. Scripture clearly reserves these offices for men, but anywhere else—ladies, you'd *better* be involved!)

Now, what about those godly men? They've got to have a good report; they've got to have an honest reputation among the people. Popularity and charisma count for nothing here. It doesn't matter if he's a TV news anchor or a millionaire or the owner of a software company. What matters here is character. What matters here is a Spirit-filled life.

"But," you ask, "what if someone has been saying things that aren't true and spreading a bad report about me? Wouldn't that unfairly disqualify me?" In my opinion, true character and integrity will shine right through one bad report. There will be others whose testimonies will override one person with a sour-grapes agenda.

...full of the Holy Spirit and wisdom...

Did you hear that? Of good report, full of the Holy Spirit, and *wise*. Some men and women have a lot of head knowledge when it comes to the Word of God, but it's never penetrated their hearts! They can quote a lot of verses and discuss seven detailed theories about the millennium, but they're not wise. As a matter of fact, when it comes to dealing with people, they're downright foolish. And God says that's not a good person to have in leadership.

During the first five years of Antioch Bible Church, I encountered some murmuring over our hiring practices. "We thought this was supposed to be a cross-cultural church!" people told me. "The only people we're hiring are white guys!"

I remember making the statement, "We will never sacrifice righteousness for skin color. We will call the best available person." The apostles didn't tell the church to select a "racially diverse" group of leaders. They didn't say anything about making the group "culturally balanced." They didn't specify young or old, rich or poor, Greek-speaking or Hebrew-speaking, educated or noneducated. There were no quotas. The only "balance" they were looking for was balanced people! The apostles simply said, "If you find people who have good reputations, good common sense, and are filled with the Spirit, you'll be okay. Let them tackle these problems while we attend to the Word."

The church is not doing well today because we wouldn't handle the problem that way.

But we will give ourselves continually to prayer, and to the ministry of the word (6:4).

What was the whole focus of the new church? What keeps coming back again and again? The Word.

The Word was more important than the distribution of food. The Word was more important than the exercise of miracles or sign gifts. If there were sign gifts, they were intended to draw people into the Word.

If there were healings, they were to attract people to the Message. If someone was raised from the dead, it was to point more and more people toward the Truth, the Word of God. The whole center is the Word, because it is the written Word that reveals the living Word and the only means of salvation.

So these church elders said, "We've got two big jobs and we're going to get them done, no matter what else is undone. We're going to preach the Word and we're going to pray."

THREE WAYS TO GET RID OF MURMURING

Do you want to know how to get rid of murmuring in the church? Verse 4 gives us two ways, and verses 5 and 6 give us a third way! Check this out:

But we will give ourselves continually to prayer....

Yes! That is *always* step number one.

1. Give yourselves to prayer.

When you're faced with murmuring in a church, call people to pray. That's the first priority. You don't need to bathe yourself in the problem. You don't need to work yourself up into a lather over the problem. You don't need to become anxious and distraught over the problem. You don't even need to spend that much time on the problem.

Not until you've prayed!

You need to recognize murmuring for what it is: an attack of the enemy who would love to bring down the church from the inside out if he can't do it from the outside in. Pray about the situation. Pray about the people. Pray for Holy Spirit wisdom. Pray for deliverance. Pray for enlightenment from the Word. Pray for godly people who could be involved in solving the problem.

The bottom line: take all these potential negatives to the Lord so that you can concentrate on positive ministry. Complaints and bickering and people problems can sap the life out of any fellowship. We'll spend more time on the negative in the ministry than we ever will on the good things that are happening among us. What we need to do is pray.

Paul summed it up like this: "Be anxious for nothing, but in every-thing, by prayer and supplication with thanksgiving, let your requests be made known unto God. And the peace of God, which passeth all understanding, shall keep your hearts and minds through Christ Jesus" (Philippians 4:6–7).

2. Stay focused on the Word.

Never become distracted from the primary by the secondary. Never allow yourself to be turned aside from the preaching and teaching of God's Word. The very answers you need for those pressing questions are in the Book! God's Word will

Bickering and people problems can sap the life out of any fellowship.

equip us for every good work (2 Timothy 3:16). God's Word is a lamp to our feet and a light to our path (Psalm 119:105). Without that light, we're only stumbling in the dark. When you've lost some-thing in your room, do you turn off the light to go look for it? No, without that light, you'll never find anything! And with-out the counsel of God's Word, we'll never solve those nagging people problems. We'll only go around and around and around. We'll be just like the children of Israel wandering in the wilderness: "Haven't I already seen that same ugly bush seventeen times this month?"

But there's one additional method for handling murmuring in this passage:

And the saying pleased the whole multitude; and they chose Stephen, a man full of faith and of the Holy Spirit, and Philip, and Prochorus, and Nicanor, and Timon, and Parmenas, and Nicolas, a proselyte of Antioch, whom they set before the apostles; and when they had prayed, they laid their hands on them (6:5).

3. Give the complainers the job they're complaining about!

There's something very interesting about those names listed in Acts 6:5. Every one of those names is a Greek name. Every one of the men selected was a Hellenistic Jew or proselyte. The church didn't name a "balanced" group at all; they were all Hellenists. And these were the very folks who had brought the problem to the table to begin with!

Most of the churches I know wouldn't handle the situation like that. Instead, the first thing we want to do is set up a committee on how to deal with this or that negative among us. By forming a committee, we're saying, "This is something we should *all* be concerned with; this is something we should *all* pay attention to." That's where the distraction comes in! That's what starts us looking inward at ourselves instead of outward at the ministry opportunities.

I think we ought to do what the early church did in this situation: When you've got someone concerned and anxious about a situation, give *them* the job to come up with some recommendations! In other words, if you've got a problem with the way something's working around here, it's your job to make it better. After all, God has already given you a heart for this aspect of the ministry. So instead of murmuring, roll up your sleeves and get busy in the Lord's work!

Now, the church needs to make sure that godly leadership oversees these efforts, but the footwork belongs to those who have the concern. Do you know how little murmuring you'd hear in the church when word got around that you've got to put some *responsibility* behind your mouth? We'd be saying, "Whoa! Where did all those complaints go?"

WHAT KEPT THE CHURCH GROWING?

And the word of the God increased, and the number of the disciples multiplied in Jerusalem greatly; and a great company of the priests were obedient to the faith (6:7).

The power of God was moving through Jerusalem like a hurricane, and even "a great company" of the Jewish priests were coming to know the Lord. I've got a question for you. Was the church multiplying, and people coming to the Lord, because they were taking care of the problem of the widows and the prejudice?

I don't think so! Why was the church still growing? Because they were praying and they were teaching the Word. Why don't we try that when we have cultural differences? Why don't we try praying and teaching the Word when we have communication gaps, when we have a generation gap, when we have a worship styles gap? Why don't we try going to our knees as a church, and going to the Word like men and women just starving for a good, solid meal?

WEAKNESS BY DIVISION

And Stephen, full of faith and power, did great wonders and signs among the people. Then there arose some from what is called the Synagogue of the Freedmen (Cyrenians, Alexandrians, and those from Cilicia and Asia), disputing with Stephen. And they were not able to resist the wisdom and the Spirit by which he spoke (6:8–10, NKJV).

Philip's job was to evangelize. Stephen's job was given to defend the gospel.

The situation described in these verses came about as the church was meeting in various synagogues around the city because it was growing like wildfire. Different brothers would teach the Word of God in these various synagogues and sometimes have debates with the synagogue leaders.

Now this incident began at a place called the Synagogue of the Freedmen. Stephen began preaching Christ to them, and, as usual, the synagogue leaders began throwing questions at him, expecting to discredit him or trip him up. But they couldn't get anywhere! The more he talked and answered their questions, the more the whole thing made sense. They couldn't resist his wisdom. They couldn't fault his logic. In reality, they couldn't refute the Holy Spirit, who filled Stephen to overflowing. And day after day, Stephen was just smokin' them!

Their solution? They tore a big page right out of Satan's book: lies and slander. They recruited men to make false charges against Stephen because they knew they couldn't make any real ones stick.

Was that fair?

No way. There was nothing fair about it. It was horribly *unfair*. It would get so unfair that an innocent man would be dragged out of the city by a mob and stoned to death just for teaching the truth about Jesus! How "unfair" can you get? The fact is (and I don't want to shock you here), the world isn't going to treat you fairly if you belong to Jesus Christ. You won't get fair media coverage. You won't get a fair hearing. You won't get equal time. You won't get an even break. *The Lord never told us that life would be fair!* But hear me: Unless we learn how to deal with unfairness within the body of Christ, how will we ever become warriors for Christ in the world? If we can't handle a few inequities within the family of God, what's going to happen to us when we're called upon to face persecution from a hostile world?

It reminds me of what the Lord once said to Jeremiah: "If you have raced with men on foot and they have worn you out, how can you compete with horses? If you stumble in safe country, how will you manage in the thickets by the Jordan?" (Jeremiah 12:5, NIV)

But check this out. Isn't it interesting that at the very same moment the church was dealing with the "fairness issue" inside the church, this unfair situation with Stephen was coming at them from the outside?

Were they ready to deal with both of them at the same time? Do you think that might have been a two-pronged attack from Satan? Do you think it's possible the church might have been a little distracted?

And all that sat in the council, looking steadfastly on him, saw his face as it had been the face of an angel (6:15).

I want to tell you a little secret. Having the face of an angel won't keep you from getting killed. Living the life of a saint won't keep the rocks from flying. Being a good neighbor and an honest citizen and a jolly good fellow won't keep you from being persecuted for Jesus Christ.

But here's the point that haunts me. What is the difference between Stephen being taken prisoner here in Acts 6 and the apostles being taken prisoner in Acts 5? Do you see a difference? Here's something that occurred to me recently: up until Acts 6, there was no disunity in the church. There was no murmuring; they were all of one heart and "one accord," as the King James puts it.

And what was the result? When Peter and John were preaching in the temple in Acts 5, the soldiers were actually afraid to put hands on them and arrest them! The captain and his officers saw the whole church gathered there, in strength and unity, and were afraid *they* might be the ones who would be stoned for messing with these servants of God.

But where is the church in Acts 6?

Where are those standing with Stephen? Why weren't Stephen's enemies afraid to pick up a rock and spill this young man's blood? Why wasn't the mob afraid to put this wonderful, radiant believer to death? Could it be that the believers in Jerusalem were so preoccupied with themselves and the murmuring and the "unfair" situation in their midst that they missed an opportunity to stand with Stephen?

We can't say for sure. But from the context, it looks like a possibility.

One thing I do know for certain is this: When the church begins to divide itself and preoccupy itself with murmuring, we lose strength. We lose clout. The world sneers at us and doesn't take us as seriously. When we start thinking about how unfair my group is being treated in the body of Christ, or my gender is being treated, or my special interests are being treated, we lose focus. We begin to major on the minors, and our influence in the world evaporates like water on a hot sidewalk.

What happens? We begin to look inward and forget about those brothers and sisters around the world who really *are* being treated unfairly and persecuted. While the church in Jerusalem was caught up with the "fairness to the widows" debate, Stephen was seized and dragged before the council. They killed him before the church could get itself turned around.

It's the same today. While congregations argue over the color of the carpet and how many hymns we sing versus how many choruses and whether my translation of the Bible is more accurate than your translation, believers around the world are being tortured and sold into slavery and slaughtered for their belief in Jesus Christ.

Where's our focus going to be, church?

While we were dividing and subdividing our denominations in America, prayer was banished from our public schools.

While we were attacking one another in seminaries, magazines, and on the airwaves, abortion on demand became the law of our land.

Church, we need to wake up and start being men and women of God. We need to quit being so culturally-sensitive and gender-sensitive and this-sensitive and that-sensitive and get back to the basics: ministering the Word of God and advancing on our knees.

The truth is, we advance together...or we don't advance at all.

BECAUSE WE'RE AFRAID OF CHURCH DISCIPLINE

I n Acts 5, the church was shaking Jerusalem like a little tree in a Texas windstorm. Everyone felt it. You couldn't miss it! The impact was huge.

And just when it looked as if that impact was in danger of serious compromise, the Holy Spirit stepped in with some drastic measures—and the impact became even greater still.

Today the church has lost much of its influence on our culture. If we are "salt," we are very, very diluted… hardly salty at all. If we are light, we are very, very dim—like a flashlight running on depleted batteries. And a very big reason for that dilution and depletion, I believe, is the church's refusal to take her purity seriously. We're afraid and intimidated by the prospect

In the name of "sensitivity," we have forfeited our opportunity for impact.

of church discipline. As a result, we've sacrificed more power than we can begin to imagine. In the name of "love and sensitivity," we have forfeited our opportunity for impact.

Acts 5 represents a crossroads in the New Testament church, at the dawning of the church age. Let's pick up Dr. Luke's narrative with the closing verses of chapter 4.

And Joseph, who by the apostles was surnamed Barnabas (which is, being interpreted, The son of consolation), a

Levite of the country of Cyprus, having land, sold it, and brought the money, and laid it at the apostles' feet.

But a certain man named Ananias, with Sapphira, his wife, sold a possession, and kept back part of the price, his wife also knowing of it, and brought a certain part, and laid it at the apostles' feet (4:36–5:2).

Acts 5:1 begins with the word "but." It points to a contrast between the heart of Barnabas and the hearts of Ananias and Sapphira. There is a very important difference between Barnabas and his giving and Ananias and Sapphira and their giving.

But Peter said, Ananias, why hath Satan filled thine heart to lie to the Holy Spirit, and to keep back part of the price of the land? (5:3)

We've lost power in the church today because we've got too many Christians in our midst with the power of Satan in them—filling their hearts!

While it remained, was it not thine own? And after it was sold, was it not in thine own power? Why has thou conceived this thing in thine heart? Thou has not lied unto men, but unto God. And Ananias, hearing these words, fell down, and died; and great fear came on all them that heard these things (5:4–5).

Now *that's* an understatement! Do you suppose there was a little soul-searching and confessing and repenting going on in the church that night? Hmmm? What is the purpose for church discipline? It is for the church as a whole to realize, "Wow! That could happen to me! God must take these matters seriously!"

And the young men arose, wrapped him up, and carried him out, and buried him. And it was about the space of three hours after, when his wife, not knowing what was done, came in. And Peter answered her, Tell me whether ye sold the land for so much? And she said, Yea, for so much (5:6–8).

Mutual sin in the church today is unbelievable. Christians who are trying to dodge discipline have a tendency to look for other believers who are also doing wrong. And they say to one another, "I know how you're struggling in your 'problem area,' so you must understand how I am struggling in my 'problem area.' I have compassion for poor you, so I know you must have compassion for poor me!"

But it isn't "a struggle" and it isn't "a problem." It is *sin*. And our so-called compassion for one another is the very opposite of true accountability; it is mutual consent to sin. (Because—after all—true accountability is *very* uncomfortable, and we don't like to be uncomfortable. Especially in church!)

THE "SIGN" NOBODY WANTS

Then Peter said unto her, How is it that ye have agreed together to test the Spirit of the Lord? Behold, the feet of them who have buried thy husband are at the door, and shall carry thee out. Then fell she down immediately at his feet, and died; and the young men came in, and found her dead, and carrying her forth, buried her by her husband. And great fear came upon all the church, and upon as many as heard these things (5:9–11).

I would think so!

Now check this out. There had been three signs in the book of Acts to this point. Each sign had been followed by a sermon,

Our so-called compassion is the very opposite of true accountability.

with an ingathering of people into the church. The first sign was tongues; after the disciples spoke in tongues and Peter delivered his message, three thousand were added to the church. The second sign was a healing at the temple, which was also followed by a sermon. This resulted in five thousand who were added to the church. The third sign was a killing, and there were so many people added to the church they couldn't even count them.

> And believers were the more added to the Lord, multitudes both of men and women (5:14).

Now isn't it amazing that God used three different signs to add to His church, and the third sign brought more people (multitudes!) than the first two. But what is it we hear people asking for today when they want to see "signs and wonders" in the church? Tongues and healings! You don't see anybody asking for a killing! That would put a whole new meaning to "slain in the Spirit," wouldn't it?

The truth is, none of these signs and wonders brought anyone to Christ. What they did was to gather a crowd for the preaching of the Word of God. The miraculous signs validated the message of the apostles—creating fear and awe. But it is the truth of the Word of God that saves.

WHY DID THEY DO IT?

Ananias and Sapphira lied and deceived because they wanted to look like Barnabas. This greathearted man from Cyprus had sold his land and brought everything he had and laid it at the apostles' feet. "Let me encourage the church with this gift," he was saying by his actions. "It's all I've got."

This couple had watched how the apostles and people in the fellowship reacted to Barnabas because of his generous gift. Barnabas wasn't looking for strokes, but he probably got 'em anyway. People were encouraged and told him so! People talked about him, smiled at him on the street, and spoke respectfully to him.

Now, honestly, we all enjoy that kind of respect, don't we? We like to have people think well of us. We like to be liked. But many times, we're not willing to pay the price for that respect and honor. We want the end result of a righteous and godly life, but we don't want to go through the process it takes to get there. We want to wear a Super Bowl ring but we don't want to train for months and years or have very large people hit us out on the field. We want the degree without paying the tuition. So we look for a shortcut.

That's what these two did. When Ananias and Sapphira saw how the Consolation Kid was being treated, they decided it would be very pleasant to receive the same treatment.

But what would it cost?

How much money?

How big of a lie?

They wanted to be honored like Barnabas, so they tried to act like him. They went

God already has the originals. He doesn't need cheap photocopies.

through the motions. That's a lot like you and me sometimes, isn't it? We know how to act, but sometimes fall short of the commitment to *become*. Now, if you and I want to be a man like Barnabas or a woman like godly Tabitha in Acts 9, we have to become righteous as they were righteous. We have to walk in the Spirit as they walked in the Spirit. It isn't just some kind of pretend game. It isn't charades. It's being inspired by a good man or a good woman's example and seeking to emulate it with all of our heart. It's much, much more than wearing the same kind of clothes, copying the same kind of mannerisms, or carrying the same kind of Bible.

Listen, God already has the originals; He doesn't need any cheap photocopies. And you and I can be "originals" too, if we are filled with the Spirit and exercise our spiritual gifts.

Hypocrisy and deceit are a major scandal in the sight of God. God *hates* a lying tongue! (see Proverbs 6:16–19) Scripture says it's an abomination to Him. We need to "speak truth, one to another." No false love. No false unity. No false flattery. No false spirituality. No saying one thing to a person's face and another thing behind his back. We need truth, truth, truth, spoken in love, love, love. Hypocrisy neutralizes the impact of the church.

WATCH THAT LEAVEN!

The church has lost power today because we are not disciplining the way God has called us to discipline…and the purity of the bride of Christ has been compromised.

God has told us over and over again what "a little leaven" can do. And we've got so much leaven in the dough these days we can't even see the dough! Here's how Paul uses that word picture for sin, in the context of church discipline:

> It is actually reported that there is sexual immorality among you, and such sexual immorality as is not even named among the Gentiles—that a man has his father's wife! And you are puffed up, and have not rather mourned, that he who has done this deed might be taken away from among you…. Your glorying is not good. Do you not know that a little leaven leavens the whole lump?

Therefore purge out the old leaven, that you may be a new lump, since you truly are unleavened (1 Corinthians 5:1–2, 6–7, NKJV).

Another translation says: "Don't you know that a little yeast works through the whole batch of dough? Get rid of the old yeast that you may be a new batch without yeast—as you really are" (5:6–7, NIV).

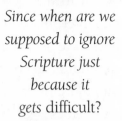

Since when are we supposed to ignore Scripture just because it gets difficult?

Leaven—or yeast—is a common biblical picture for sin. It doesn't take much time and it doesn't take much leaven to ferment a whole batch of dough. And it doesn't take much tolerance of sin in a body of believers to work its way through that whole body—affecting every person. The result is a removal of God's hand of blessing from that local assembly—and a diminished impact on the community.

Yes, it is very difficult to exercise biblical discipline in today's church. But that doesn't mean we should walk away from the Lord's command. Since when are we supposed to ignore Scripture just because it gets *difficult?*

Yes, people can (and do) say: "Well, if I'm going to get disciplined here, I'll just go somewhere else and start over. I don't have to put up with this grief and humiliation. Some new church will accept me. Some new fellowship will love me. They'll appreciate my tithe. They won't get in my face or embarrass me. I'm outta here!"

It stung. It hurt. And it worked. The man repented.

That man in 1 Corinthians 5 didn't have such an option! There weren't "31 flavors" of churches in his town; he couldn't shop for a different church the way you and I shop grocery stores for the best bargains. As a result, when the Corinthian church finally did exercise discipline at Paul's urging, that man felt its bite. It stung. It hurt. And it *worked*. He repented of his sin, and Paul urged the brothers and sisters to welcome him back with open arms (see 2 Corinthians 2:1–8).

Just a few months prior to the release of this book, there was a rally of over sixty-five churches on the shore of Lake Washington on Seattle's east side to address (among other things) that very issue. With over 20,000 church members and attenders standing together in that place, we proclaimed our common belief in the literal interpretation of Scripture and our unity in the Lord's commands. We served notice that there would be no more running from church to church to escape biblical discipline. There would be no more pitting of one Bible-believing church against another.

Our message? If you're disciplined in one church and try to run to another with the matter unresolved, then you will have *two* churches involved in your discipline!

We determined together on that day that this is a *biblical* issue—and one we must deal with if we want to see our city shaken to its core for Jesus Christ. We need to return to a mutual commitment to purity: leadership holding the people to biblical standards of purity, and people holding the leadership to the very same standards. We need to hold each other accountable; that's what the church is all about. I *am* my brother's keeper—and he is mine! I'll make sure you're living right, and when I find out that you're not living right, I'll call you to righteousness. Why? Because down the road I may need your strength to call *me* back to righteousness if I go off the deep end.

Tough, honest questions have a way of cutting through the fog.

But all of that healthy, mutual accountability can just fade away when we don't pursue biblical discipline as a church. If the people don't see the church leadership following the biblical pattern, they begin feeling like they "don't have a right" to call another brother or sister to accountability. And the whole procedure given to us by the Lord in Matthew 18:15–17 never even gets out of the blocks. The fact is, true accountability doesn't start with the pastors or the elders or the Sunday school teachers…it starts one on one.

But Peter said, Ananias…

The big fisherman started asking tough questions as soon as Ananias walked through the door. He asked a series of questions that began to penetrate the lie.

Tough, honest questions have a way of cutting through the fog. You and I can be intimidated or reluctant to ask those tough questions. We can suspect or even know that one of our friends is getting into some serious sin and trying to cover it over. But we don't want to "risk the friendship" by asking the hard things that need to be asked.

Don't you dare call that love or sensitivity! It is cowardice, and it is doing your friend no favor at all. Love cannot exist apart from truth. Real love springs out of truth. And when we pretend everything is the same and that nothing is wrong, it is like counseling our friend to ignore a cancerous tumor. That thing will never "go away by itself"; it needs to be surgically removed. And the longer you wait the more difficult and painful it will be.

In this case, silence is not "golden." It is poison.

If someone comes to the leadership here at Antioch Bible Church and says, "Are you aware that so and so is doing such and such?" we will say, "Have you talked to that person? You need to go to them as the Scripture says. If they don't want to listen to you, grab a brother or a sister and go talk to them again. If they still don't want to listen, then it's time for church leadership to get involved—more than once—to seek to persuade them to change their direction. If they don't repent then, we will bring them before the church, tell their sin publicly, describe our efforts to get them to repent, and tell them that we are withdrawing fellowship from them."

Deliverate blindness eliminates power. It makes a church anemic.

From that time forward, until they repent, the congregation must no longer treat them like a believer.

What, then, does repentance mean? Repentance means admitting I am wrong, and making up my mind to turn 180 degrees from the direction I've been going—and it's not an option to go back that way again.

But this whole process of accountability and church discipline requires going below surface level in each other's lives. It requires us to get involved on a deeper level with each other…and that's uncomfortable for us. Oh, but when the process works the way it's supposed to work…when someone truly submits to the discipline, repents from the heart, and asks and receives forgiveness from the church…that's *powerful*.

That's *healing*.

That's *joyful*.

That's *humbling* for all of us.

Instead of something being swept under the rug, it's dealt with, just as Scripture says to deal with it. The decay or leaven in the church is because of sin that's never been dealt with—sin that's been covered over. We try to talk about righteousness, but it stinks inside the church because we know what's going on behind closed doors and we aren't saying anything!

That deliberate blindness eliminates power. It makes a church very, very weak and anemic.

I am personally determined that I will never give up the power to pray by not having a clear conscience.

That's what the church needs to say. We are not willing to give up a clear conscience and the power to pray and worship God out of reluctance to confront sin. Because how in the world can you worship God when you know you've got a lie sitting behind you? That's what makes our worship so weak! Because there is no call to purity and righteousness in the presence of a holy and awesome God.

GUARDING THE INFANT CHURCH

Great fear came upon all the church, and upon as many as heard these things (5:11).

Why did the Holy Spirit act so quickly and decisively in this instance? If He acted the same way today, putting to death those who are guilty of hypocrisy, there would have to be a morgue in every church basement. Why did He move in this particular circumstance?

I believe it was because the church was so new. This was the dawning of a new era. The church was very young, tender, malleable. Satan wanted to corrupt and compromise the church before it ever had a chance to spread out of Jerusalem and sink its roots into cities such as Antioch of Syria. So He was standing guard over the infant church, until that time when it could become more firmly established.

It's been extremely uncomfortable at times. We shouldn't expect otherwise!

When hypocrisy raised its head in the persons of Ananias and Sapphira, God killed them right on the spot.

And *fear* came on the church.

It wasn't comfortable, friend. But let me tell you…it was very effective.

Let's just visualize how that might look today. Imagine I'm up on the platform on Sunday morning, preaching. But suddenly I push my Bible aside and say, "Look, I know the Bible teaches so and so, but I don't believe what the Bible says. Now, let me tell you what life is *really* like." And I start preaching some heresy right here in front of the congregation. But before I can get really warmed up—boom!—I just fall over dead!

Right away I know I've got the ushers worried, because they would be thinking, "How are we going to pick him up? Man, we'll break our backs hauling him off that platform."

But I have a pretty good idea there would be some new fear in this part of the world about misinterpreting the Scriptures. There would be some pastors staying up all night on Saturday night to make sure that their messages were true to the Word. There would be some Sunday school teachers and Bible study leaders who would be taking their lessons just a tad more seriously, don't you think so?

Our church here in Bellevue, Antioch Bible Church, has committed to following through on the discipline process...come what may. And we've had people angry at us. We've had people blast our leadership and threaten lawsuits. People have accused me personally of being unloving, judgmental, and insensitive.

Comfortable? No way. It's been extremely uncomfortable at times. We shouldn't expect it to be otherwise! I'll say it again, God never promised us that church would be comfortable. God never promised us that the Christian life would be comfortable. There's a reason why most people choose the broad road to hell than the narrow road to righteousness: It's easier! It's more comfortable (at least for a while). But today's culture thinks church ought to be nice and warm and comforting and accepting all the time. We've gotten so far from God's standards that now holding each other to righteousness has become "condemning," "judgmental," "insensitive," and "unloving."

People who are confronted with unrighteousness often say, "How can you judge me? After all, God is love. He has open arms. He is forgiving. He wouldn't treat me the way you're trying to treat me. None of the other churches would treat me this way!" The problem today is that people who are caught in sin think the church ought to be loving and accepting *without qualification.* They want the church to be like some kind of doting grandfather who winks at sin and says, "Well, boys will be boys" (And girls will be girls, too!). But their idea of "loving" has totally removed itself from true biblical love.

Their idea of "loving" has totally removed itself from true biblical love.

We've reshaped God into our own image and imagine that He will not hold us accountable to righteousness, but that He will "understand our situation" and in His "love" He will be tolerant of our rebellion.

God does not judge on a curve! As J. Vernon McGee used to say, "You're either a saint or you ain't!"

There is just as much biblical love in rejection as there is in acceptance. But that's hard for our contemporary culture to understand. The truth of the matter is this: If the church turns you away because of your refusal to repent, it is the strongest demonstration of love they could possibly show you. How else could we help you to wake up before Satan has you completely under his clutches? In Luke it tells us that the whole heavens rejoice when one sinner repents.

But we miss that joy because we won't participate in the process. Instead of doing what Scripture says, we tend to put our arms around the unrepentant person and say, "Oh, you're okay. You're just going through a rough time in your life." No, he's not—he's sinning! And he needs to be disciplined! He needs to repent.

But why should someone turn if there are no visible repercussions to their sin? The average Christian is too immature to embrace repentance apart from discipline.

We're more afraid of people and the ACLU than we are of God!

In spite of all of this, the church remains afraid to discipline. Afraid of people's displeasure. Afraid of being sued. Afraid of the ACLU. We're more afraid of people and the ACLU than we are of God!

Hebrews 12 says, "Hey, you can't be a child of God without the Father's discipline."

> And you have forgotten the exhortation which speaks to you as to sons: "My son, do not despise the chastening of the LORD, nor be discouraged when you are rebuked by Him; for whom the LORD loves He chastens, and scourges every son whom He receives." If you endure chastening, God deals with you as with sons; for what son is there whom a father does not chasten? But if you are without chastening, of which all have become partakers, then you are illegitimate and not sons. Furthermore, we have had human fathers who corrected us, and we paid them respect. Shall we not much more readily be in subjection to the Father of spirits and live? For they indeed for a few days chastened us as seemed best to them, but He for our profit, that we may be partakers of His holiness (Hebrews 12:5–10, NKJV).

If the world never sees the church holding people accountable and disciplining its members—and the church is supposed to be His reflection on earth—then it must follow that God doesn't hold people accountable or discipline them either! Could that be part of the reason for the great moral slide in our nation?

We need to look diligently into this matter because it will affect other people in the body. We're kidding ourselves if we think that it won't.

The writer to the Hebrews goes on to give this warning:

Pursue peace with all people, and holiness, without which no one will see the Lord: looking carefully lest anyone fall short of the grace of God; lest any root of bitterness springing up cause trouble, and by this many become defiled... (Hebrews 12:14–15, NKJV).

Pursue accountability! Pursue it diligently! Watch out for the poison roots that spread the poison to others.

But exhort one another daily, while it is called "Today," lest any of you be hardened through the deceitfulness of sin (Hebrews 3:13, NKJV).

The true path to joy and healing is a hard road to follow sometimes. It can be steep. It can be narrow. It can be lonely. But it beats the alternative a million times over.

BECAUSE WE AREN'T FOLLOWING THE BIBLICAL PATTERN

PART 1

I magine with me that the dishwasher in the Hutcherson manor was broken (scary thought!) and that I wanted to find out how to fix it (scarier thought!). What would be my first step?

Well, I guess the first thing I'd do is go visit my favorite Dodge truck dealer. I like looking at Dodge pickups—especially really big, ebony black ones—and I could just wander into the service department, have a cup of coffee, and ask the guys about my Westinghouse dishwasher.

Now, what are they going to do? They're going to be very concerned that I am no longer mentally competent. They're going to think I took one too many hits from those offensive linemen in my pro career. And then they're going to quietly and discreetly call the police, because if you've got a guy *my* size who's acting nuts, there could be some havoc in there after a while if I don't get some answers!

Obviously, if I want help with the dishwasher (which I'm not sure I do, because if I learn how it works, I might have to *use* it), I need to consult the Westinghouse instruction manual. After all, it came with the dishwasher, all sealed up in a nice plastic bag.

But a lot of us men don't like manuals; we feel that we ought to be able to do the job with our own two hands and agile mind. You can observe this behavior most often around Christmastime, when we dads go to work putting together things like new bicycles and trikes and swingsets. Instructions? Who needs 'em? A real man ought to be able to figure these things out.

And then when we've got that shiny new bike all put together, we find ourselves looking at some extra pieces. Wasn't that nice of those manufacturers to throw in some extra parts—just in case something broke?

But what happens when we road test that little beauty? The bike goes in two different directions and the kid goes in a third. Now we're forced to open up that plastic bag and fish out the instruction manual. Well, what do you know! Those extra parts weren't there just because of the manufacturer's generosity. They were there because we *needed* them to make that thing work right.

We can't find many churches today that resemble the original article.

Now, if we're smart enough to consult the instruction manual when we find ourselves over our heads and beyond our mechanical ability…what do we do when the church isn't functioning the way it ought to be functioning? Doesn't it follow that we should go to the Instruction Manual, the Word of God? Doesn't it make sense to research the biblical pattern and try to line up with that?

We wonder today why the church seems so weak and anemic.

We wonder today why the church hasn't been able to stop or even slow the moral free fall in our country and the frightening disintegration of our culture.

We wonder why we haven't been able to shake up the cities where we are living and draw the lost and the unchurched to a saving knowledge of Christ.

I believe it is because we have not followed the biblical pattern, which God has promised to bless. We haven't consulted the Manual, or, if we have, we have consulted the Manual *selectively,* leaving out some major emphases of Scripture.

WHAT HAPPENED TO THE REAL DEAL?

We look at the contemporary church and we think church is *supposed* to look that way. As far back as we can remember, it's *always* looked that way. But if we read the Instruction Manual about what the New Testament church really looks like, we can't find very many churches today that resemble the original article.

The model church in Antioch had *everybody* in it.

> Now there were in the church that was at Antioch certain prophets and teachers, as Barnabas, and Symeon, who was called Niger... (13:1).

A literal translation of this latter man's name might read: "Symeon called the black." Isn't that great? Now, Matthew Henry says the reason why they called him "Symeon the black" was because of his *hair* color. I don't think so! In my studies, I've become convinced that Symeon was from north Africa.

The model church in Antioch had everybody in it.

The Black Man.

Now, that happens to be my nickname, too. "Black Man." Friends who are real close to me say, "Hey Black Man, how's it goin'?" People that don't know me say, "Hey Black Man," and they get black eyes!

From my studies in Acts and the book of Mark, I believe Symeon to be the very same person as Simon, the Cyrenian who was yanked out of the crowds and forced to carry the cross of Jesus Christ, in Mark 15:1.

Now, do you think being compelled to walk with Jesus to Calvary and carry His cross for Him might have made a little bit of an impression on this man? And in the eleven to twelve years following the crucifixion, he would have had time to embrace the Lord as Savior in Jerusalem and grow in his maturity.

When the persecution hit the church in Jerusalem, note what Dr. Luke says in Acts 11:19–20:

Now they who were scattered abroad upon the persecution that arose about Stephen, traveled as far as Phoenicia, and Cyprus, and Antioch, preaching the word to none but unto the Jews only. And some of them were men of Cyprus and Cyrene, who, when they were come to Antioch, spoke unto the Greeks, preaching the Lord Jesus.

I believe Symeon (Simon) was one of those men from Cyrene who went to Antioch, began preaching to the Gentiles, and helped found that wide-open, on-fire church which became the very model of all New Testament churches to follow.

...and Lucius of Cyrene, and Manaen, who had been brought up with Herod, the tetrarch, and Saul. As they ministered to the Lord, and fasted, the Holy Spirit said, Separate me Barnabas and Saul for the work unto which I have called them (13:1–2).

As we peek through the church window at Antioch, who do we see? We see Barnabas, a Jew from Cyprus. We see Paul, a former Pharisee and church persecutor. We see Symeon, a man from north Africa, and one of the church leaders. We see Romans. We see other Gentiles.

God painted the church at Antioch with a full palette.

God painted the church at Antioch with a full palette. What we see is a dynamic blend of cultures and races—and the place was exploding with life!

But most churches in our country today don't have that kind

of color scheme or blend of cultures. We've gone backwards. We've gone back to homogeneous, one-race, one-nationality, one-culture churches. We've become "comfortable" with that arrangement; but it is not what God intended, and I do not believe the Lord of the church is pleased.

If we're not following the Manual, we can get so far off track and see something happening the wrong way for so long that we convince ourselves that it's right!

I recently heard a true story about a Midwest fish market that had such trouble getting in fresh fish that they proclaimed bad fish a "delicacy" and sold them at inflated prices. Now, that's good marketing, but do you know what? Bad fish are still bad fish. And unbiblical practices are still unbiblical practices, no matter how much tartar sauce we put on them or how long we've been swallowing them.

Why has today's church lost power? Because with every generation we're getting further away from the original design. We're getting further and further from what we are supposed to be...what we were meant to be!

As we've already established, all-white churches, all-black churches, all-*anything* churches don't line up with the biblical pattern. And can we really afford to compromise the biblical standard in any of our practices? We have adjusted to being "comfortable" (with our own kind) instead of being righteous. Now, if you want to be comfortable, you're doing a great job! But if you want to line up with Scripture, then you're off base, regardless of how "good" it looks.

After all, the Mormon cult "looks good" from the outside. Their buildings look good. Their books look good. Their people look good. Their colleges and universities look good. Their temple and their choir are looking good. They're growing! They're sending out thousands of missionaries. Their coffers are filled. The only problem is, they're going against the Word of God. They don't line up with Scripture—they make up their own!

As the true church of Jesus Christ, we need to say, "We're going to do it according to the Manual or we're going to shut the door."

Let's say you're a dad, and you've given your teenage son a job to do. You tell him, "I want you to go pick up the wood that's lying around the barn and stack it alongside the barn."

"We're going to do it according to the Manual... or shut the door!"

But instead of doing what you've asked, your son goes out and gathers wood around the garage and stacks it by the garage. After a few hours he comes to you and says, "Dad, I'm finished. With sensitivity to your directions and a desire to please you, I have done what you've asked. I have picked up the wood around the garage, and I have stacked it. Now can I go to the football game?"

And what do you say as a dad?

He did his job with a smile. He did his job quickly. But he didn't do the thing you'd asked!

And in the same way, we say to God, "God, would You please bless this ministry? God, we want to rock this city for You! God, please show Your power among us." But God says, "Why are you asking Me for those things when you haven't done what I've asked you to do? *Stack the wood at the barn!*"

Why have we separated the body of Christ, in violation of the biblical pattern? If the world today could see blacks and whites and Hispanics and Asians all worshiping together in one place with one spirit, they would say, "Now *this* is something supernatural." Or, as the magicians who watched Moses said to Pharaoh, "This is the finger of God!"

When you look at the Old Testament, you have to ask yourself, Why would the nations around Israel want to worship the one true God when the tribes of Israel were always warring with each other? As far as the watching nations were concerned, it was "the same old same old." And why should the world be impressed when it sees the church of Jesus Christ even more segregated and divided than what they see every day in the workplace?

The pattern is pretty simple. God has changed, but man doesn't want to change. God wants men and women from all cultures and backgrounds to come together in one body. Man wants to separate. Man wants to draw distinctions between people. Man wants to isolate according to differences. But what does the Scripture say?

> For there is no difference between the Jew and the Greek; for the same Lord over all is rich unto all that call upon him (Romans 10:12).
>
> There is neither Jew nor Greek, there is neither slave nor free, there is neither male nor female; for you are all one in Christ Jesus...and heirs according to the promise (Galatians 3:28, 29, NKJV).
>
> There is neither Greek nor Jew, circumcised nor uncircumcised, barbarian, Scythian, slave nor free, but Christ is all and in all (Colossians 3:11, NKJV).
>
> For he himself [Jesus] is our peace, who has made the two one and has destroyed the barrier, the dividing wall of hostility (Ephesians 2:14, NIV).

One body.
One church.
One faith.
One Lord.

One. One. One. No separation! No making distinctions!

That's the biblical pattern. Blacks laboring alongside Asians. Messianic Jews working alongside Native Americans. Anglos working alongside Latinos. Everyone contributing his or her spiritual gift and unique cultural heritage for the common good.

You still think I'm making too much of this?

Please remember what happened when Peter and Barnabas and some of the Jewish folk visited Antioch and drew apart from the brothers and sisters to eat by themselves. Was it a big deal? It was a *very* big deal. It was a major scandal in the church. So much so that it brought two apostles head to head.

> When Peter came to Antioch, I opposed him to his face, because he was clearly in the wrong. Before certain men came from James, he used to eat with the Gentiles. But when they arrived, he began to draw back and separate himself from the Gentiles because he was afraid of those who belonged to the circumcision group. The other Jews joined him in his hypocrisy, so that by their hypocrisy even Barnabas was led astray. *When I saw that they were not acting in line with the truth of the gospel,* I said to Peter in front of them all... (Galatians 2:11–14, NIV).

God's new model was the Antioch model. God's new pattern for the church was the Antioch pattern. And when the Jews from Jerusalem who were visiting Antioch started moving backwards, separating themselves according to old traditions, Paul let loose a bolt of apostolic wrath! Why? Because "I saw that they were not acting with the truth of the gospel."

Now, obviously Paul was concerned about the church turning back to the old Jewish system of following the law rather than salvation by grace through faith in the Lord Jesus. But I think it was more than that. I think that the Holy Spirit wanted to emphasize His displeasure about the church of Jesus Christ slipping back into exclusivism and separatism and segregation. The issue brought Peter and Paul head to head! It may have contributed to the eventual split of Paul and Barnabas. "Drawing away" and separatism are a lot bigger deal to God than we may have thought.

Until we repent of separatism, God isn't free to bless as He might.

Until we repent of this separatism, God isn't free to bless as He might. We really don't know how much we are holding God's blessings away from the church by not living the biblical model and following the biblical pattern. And the more we get away from the biblical pattern, the less the world really knows that He is alive and well among us.

But listen, beyond all that…we're also missing the richness of what we could contribute to one another. If I have an all-white church or an all-black church, I am missing what God has put into the other group that could bless and complete and help my fellowship. I also become less sensitive. Less tolerant. Less willing to bend or stretch. Less willing to move out of my comfort zone. If I'm in a church of "all alikes," I don't have to depend on the Holy Spirit to make me sensitive to the needs of my brother or sister from a different background and culture. I am diminished! My heart is smaller!

But you say, "Hutch, you don't know my town, or my community. We don't have any minorities in our town." My reply would be, "Have you asked the Holy Spirit to open your eyes? Have you really opened your doors to the disenfranchised in your community? If you haven't, you're missing out!" And I can't emphasize enough how *much* we are missing.

THE ANTIOCH MODEL

From chapter 2 to chapter 10 of the book of Acts, the spotlight of the Holy Spirit was on the church at Jerusalem.

As God allowed persecution to press on that centralized church, the saints were dispersed. They began to do what the Lord had intended them to do all along when He said, "But ye shall receive power, after the Holy Spirit is come upon you; and ye shall be witnesses unto me both in Jerusalem, and in all Judea, and in Samaria, and unto the uttermost part of the earth" (Acts 1:8).

From chapter 11 to chapter 18 of the book of Acts, the church at Antioch is mentioned fourteen times. It becomes the center of church activity. The Holy Spirit's spotlight moves from the church at Jerusalem to remain on the church at Antioch.

If churches don't line up with God's New Testament model, who changed?

Paul's first missionary journey was launched from Antioch and culminated at Antioch. Ditto with the second missionary journey. The third also originated in Antioch. As the missionaries planted churches, they modeled them after the church from which they had been sent: Antioch.

Now, I've got a question. If churches today don't line up with the New Testament model, who changed? God has never changed from the biblical pattern established in the book of Acts. And He won't change it until there's something better.

So if we've moved from multiracial, multicultural churches to today's segregated, homogeneous fellowships, we haven't improved, have we? As a matter of fact, we're doing what God never does. We're going backwards in His plan.

God never goes back. That's what the whole book of Hebrews is about. How can you go back to the Law once you've embraced grace through faith in the Lord Jesus Christ?

He's not going to *change* the church until there is something better! And the only thing better for the church now is the Rapture, when our Lord claims His bride and takes her to heaven. That's our next step, and what could be better than that? God always goes from better to better to better.

A PATTERN FOR LEADERSHIP, TOO

And the hand of the Lord was with them [at Antioch]; and a great number believed, and turned unto the Lord. Then tidings of these things came unto the ears of the church which was in Jerusalem; and they sent forth Barnabas, that he should go as far as Antioch, who, when he came, and had seen the grace of God, was glad, and exhorted them all, that with purpose of heart they would cling unto the Lord. For he was a righteous man, and full of the Holy Spirit and of faith; and many people were added unto the Lord. Then departed Barnabas to Tarsus, to seek Saul. And when he had found him, he brought him unto Antioch. And it came to pass that a whole year they assembled themselves with the church, and taught much people. And the disciples were called Christians first in Antioch (11:21–26).

The church at Antioch was growing like a prairie fire, and there were many people—all *kinds* of people—coming to know the Lord. So the church at Jerusalem sent Barnabas to encourage them (that was his thing!) and to make sure that they had their message straight and were living according to the Word.

Barnabas was having a ball. It didn't take him long to see where the Holy Spirit had been busy! And who did Barnabas recruit to help him? He went over to Tarsus and picked up a fiery young preacher named Saul…who would become the apostle Paul. These men joined my man Symeon the black and others on the leadership team.

So what can we tell from this leadership snapshot of the church at Antioch? We can see strong, mature leaders—no matter what their heritage or background—who are willing to step into the gap to help and encourage the saints. The secret of leadership in the church, you see, is *maturity,* not color. So why is it that in so many all-Chinese churches they look for only mature Chinese believers to lead? And why do black churches look for mature African Americans to lead their people? And why do white churches choose only mature men of their own color to lead? The truth of it is, some of these leaders may not be all that mature…but they are the right color!

The secret of leadership is maturity, not color.

The church at Antioch shows us a different model. There were all kinds of people in leadership at Antioch, and I want to let you in on a little secret: All kinds of people in the leadership will attract all kinds of people in the congregation.

I've had leaders from other churches see what's happening here in our Bellevue, Washington, Antioch and say to me, "Man, we want to be cross-cultural, too." But they're not willing to open up their staff or leadership team to mature believers of all colors, and they're not willing to embrace the music or the distinctives of more than one culture.

The whole issue of the church is to do it the way God said to do it.

If you want to be cross-cultural, you need to embrace the Antioch model. And Antioch was wide open!

What is the whole issue of the church? The issue of the church is to do it the way God said to do it. If you don't do it the

New Testament way, I've got a problem with it. Why? Because I think God's got a problem with it.

BECAUSE
WE AREN'T
FOLLOWING
THE BIBLICAL
PATTERN

PART 2

I t's amazing to me that, even as believers, we can be born-again unbelievers.

(Now, why are you staring at the page like that?)

After all, when we say that we are "believers," aren't we saying that we believe the Word of God? And if we say that, it follows to my simple mind that we should pursue life the way God says to pursue it. We should model our churches after the church He sets forth in Scripture. And if we neglect or refuse to do it the way God has said to do it, then we're basically saying we don't believe that's the best way. We're become born-again unbelievers, which will always be a paradox.

Now, the question that we should ask ourselves every day—every moment of our lives, really—is, do I really want to do it God's way? That's a penetrating question; it can keep you thinking for a while. What activities should I enhance in my life if I really want to do it God's way? Or what activities or relationships should I drop in my life if I want to do it His way? What jokes should I trash? What language should I put away? What conversations should I terminate? What television programs should I get rid of? What magazines…what books…what hobbies should I let go?

Do I truly want to do it His way? All the way?

That's the kind of question that cuts deep into our personal lives. But it should also govern what we do as the church of Jesus

Christ. *His way?* Are we following traditions or practices or methods that have been passed down to us over the years, or are we seeking to line up with the teaching of God's Word? And if we find that one of our "traditions" is out of sync with the Word, what then? Do we have the courage to set the traditions of men aside?

The church at Antioch in Syria, I believe, is the New Testament model for what today's church—for what all churches—should be. It gives us the biblical pattern for a multiracial, multicultural fellowship. It also gives us the biblical pattern for sending out missionaries.

A BIBLICAL PATTERN FOR MISSIONS

Who sent out Barnabas and Paul on that first missionary journey? A mission agency? The church at Antioch? Who *initiated* the process? Look again at Acts 13:2:

> As they ministered to the Lord, and fasted, the Holy Spirit said, Separate me Barnabas and Saul for the work unto which I have called them.

When it comes time for the church to send out workers from their midst, who does the calling? The Holy Spirit. He is the One who selects both the work and the workers.

As they prayed and fasted, the Spirit moved... the Spirit called.

What was the church doing when the Holy Spirit picked these men for special service? They were fasting and, as the King James says, *ministering* to the Lord. What does that mean? They were *worshiping.* As they worshiped, the Spirit moved. As they prayed and fasted, the Spirit called. In other words, if you're going to have the Spirit intervene in your life and give you specific direction, you've got to be seeking the Lord in the way the Scriptures say to seek Him. You've got to do it the way God says to do it.

> So they, being sent forth by the Holy Spirit, departed unto Seleucia; and from there they sailed to Cyprus. And when they were at Salamis, they preached the word of God in the synagogues of the Jews; and they had also John as their helper (13:4–5).

It was a great team. They had a teacher, an encourager, and a gopher. (They told John Mark, "Go fer this, go fer that!")

But what's the underlying pattern here? God calls the church, God calls the missionaries, and *together* we send them out. In other words, if the missionary candidate is listening to God and the church is listening to God, they should get the same message because God doesn't contradict Himself.

When the Holy Spirit is involved in something, there is agreement.

Were Barnabas and Paul listening to God? Yes, they were. Was the church at Antioch listening to God? Yes, they were, too. So there was no conflict about whether or not Barnabas and Paul should go. If there had been a conflict, what would that have meant? It would have meant someone wasn't listening to God or didn't want to hear God.

I think this same principle works right across the board in life. For instance...if a husband is listening carefully to God, and a wife is listening carefully to God, there should be no conflict between them. So if there's conflict in your home as husband and wife, one of you or both of you are not listening to God! It's that simple. In the same way, if a parent is listening to God, and the children are listening to God, there should be no conflict between parents and children. Turmoil in the family—and in the family of

God—occurs when someone will not (or cannot) hear God's voice.

In the church at Antioch of Syria, there was no problem and no debate. Why? Do you suppose it might be because they started on their knees? I don't know *how* the Holy Spirit chose to speak to them as they were praying, but there was no doubt at all about what He'd said. They prayed, the Holy Spirit called, the Holy Spirit revealed, and there was no way the church could say no. There was no way the missionaries could say no, either; they had to go.

When the Holy Spirit is involved in something, there is agreement. There are times when a man will say he wants to be a missionary, but his wife is struggling with the idea. There is conflict. Somebody's not listening to God! And the church should not send them. Why destroy a marriage and blunt God's work?

Or maybe a church has a goal or a "quota" of missionaries they want to get out in a given year. When they find an available someone who seems to have an affinity and love for a certain people group, they want to put the wheels in motion. Send him! Send her! But that's not the biblical pattern. The biblical pattern is an undeniable agreement between the church and missionary candidate or couple that this is the will and desire of the Holy Spirit.

Notice something else. Barnabas and Paul hadn't just graduated from Bible school in need of a job. They weren't looking for a way to get busy in the Lord's work; they were already ministering in the local body. They were preaching and teaching and encouraging and exhorting and evangelizing. They were exercising their gifts. It was easy for the Holy Spirit to say, in effect, "I want these guys to continue doing what they're doing, but I want them to do it over *here* for a while."

These men weren't out sitting on the curb, waiting for someone to call their number. They were involved in ministry up to their eyeballs. The body already knew the value and the integrity and the effectiveness of their work, because they'd been observing it for years. Here at Antioch in Bellevue, we've tried to follow that pattern. We're not going to send someone to do ministry "somewhere else" when they haven't done diddlysquat here. "Well," someone might say, "I just feel moved to do such and such a ministry over there, and I'm not doing it here because I'm getting ready to do it over there!"

Sorry. We just won't send someone like that. We don't believe it's the biblical way. Short-term missions trips are something different, of course; everyone can benefit from an experience like that. But even so, when someone returns from a short-term missions trip, we want to see him or her busy in the body here, doing the same kinds of things, pursuing ministry with the same heart and the same passion and the same commitment. If you're not doing the Lord's work with a whole heart

These men weren't sitting out on the curb, waiting for someone to call their number.

and godly attitude here at home, sending you to Mongolia won't change a thing. And it certainly won't help Mongolia. They must have enough problems of their own without taking on one of ours!

> So they, *being sent forth by the Holy Spirit,* departed unto Seleucia. And from there they sailed to Cyprus (13:4).

Can you imagine the confidence Barnabas and Paul felt as they climbed onto that ship at Seleucia and headed for Cyprus? "Hey, we were sent by the Holy Spirit! The Holy Spirit told us He has a job for us to do. And if He's sending us, then He can take care of us all along the way."

When God sends you—and you know it in your heart of

hearts—you will have the power to endure whatever negatives or pressures or sorrows He may call upon you to face. When the church sends you without being sure of God's calling, we're asking for a failure.

Did Barnabas and Paul need that unshakable confidence of their calling in their souls? You'd better believe it! Listen for a moment to some of the "highlights" (lowlights?) of Paul's ministry in this paraphrase of 2 Corinthians 11:23–29:

I have worked harder than any of them.
I have served more prison sentences!
I have been beaten times without number.
I have faced death again and again.
I have been beaten the regulation thirty-nine stripes by the
Jews five times.
I have been beaten with rods three times.
I have been stoned once.
I have been shipwrecked three times.
I have been twenty-four hours in the open sea.

In my travels I have been in constant danger from rivers, from bandits, from my own countrymen, and from pagans. I have faced danger in city streets, danger in the desert, danger on the high seas, danger among false Christians. I have known drudgery, exhaustion, many sleepless nights, hunger and thirst, fasting, cold and exposure.

Apart from all external trials I have the daily burden of responsibility for all the churches (PHILLIPS).

A believer in that position had better not doubt his calling! A man or woman experiencing things like that had better make sure they were sent by *God,* not just by some church or mission agency!

...From there they sailed to Cyprus.

Guess who lived in Cyprus? That was Barnabas's hometown! And the first place they sent him was back home. For Barnabas, that may have been starting with the toughest place first. That's one way I as pastor can help determine whether or not someone is ready to be sent out by our church as a missionary. If I really want to know about your local ministry, I need to check with the people you're living with! If you and I can live for Christ in front of people we know, living that life in front of people we don't know won't seem hard at all. Isn't that good stuff? The Bible just takes care of everything, doesn't it?

> And when they had gone through the isle unto Paphos, they found a certain sorcerer, a false prophet, a Jew, whose name was Bar-jesus... (13:6).

Uh-oh! Opposition. Almost right out of the cracker box. They just got started on this wonderful missionary journey, with all the warm, fuzzy feelings from their send-off party, and the words of the Holy Spirit still ringing in their ears, and *boom!* Up popped a satanic sorcerer who "withstood them" and tried to turn people from the faith.

What's the deal here? Weren't they sent forth by the Lord, with the blessing of the church? Weren't they walking according to the known will of God? Yes, they were. And this opposition from Satan—uncomfortable and gut-wrenching as it might have been—ought to have reassured them that they were on the right track.

If you're truly following God's calling... you can expect opposition.

It's just a fact of life that if you're truly following God's calling and doing what He wants you to do, you can *expect* opposition from the enemy. Satan will oppose you, as we've already established, with external pressure and internal pressure and whatever other means he can devise. He'll throw bombs at you, he'll throw missiles at you, he'll throw your relatives at you, he'll throw the kitchen sink at you if he needs to. If on the other hand your life is as smooth as an alpine lake at dawn, without even a ripple breaking the surface, you'd better check your calling! If you are living for Jesus and giving the gospel of Jesus, *expect* controversy, *expect* attacks.

If Paul and Barnabas expected them and took them in stride, why shouldn't we?

Years ago, I used to get hammered in ministry and say, "Man, I just don't know why this is happening." Getting hammered in football was one thing; they *paid* guys a lot of money to hammer me...and I got to hammer back! But now I had a family—and it didn't seem fair that they were taking these shots, too.

Finally, after feeling sorry for myself for a while, it dawned on me: *Wake up, boy. Are you God's man? Are you a preacher of the gospel? If you can't handle the heat, what are you doing in ministry in the first place?* The truth of it is, I can't get OUT of the ministry unless and until God says I can get out. And when my wife stood with me at the altar and said, "I do," she stepped right into my calling with me. That's another reason to be very careful about marrying someone who has the same heart for God and His work that you do. They'll share all the rewards and the fulfillment and the joys of serving the Lord...but they'll also dodge the bricks with you.

A BIBLICAL PATTERN FOR WORSHIP

While they were worshiping the Lord and fasting... (13:2, NIV)

Worshiping

We tend to use that word lightly, don't we? We talk about "worship songs," "worship styles," "worship teams," "worship tapes," "worship leaders," and a "worship center." We follow this tradition and we follow that tradition, according to the way we've been brought up or the denomination with which we're most familiar. But the truth is, if we truly want to worship, we've got to worship according to what the Bible says worship is.

In the final analysis, it doesn't matter what your family did.

Or what part of the country you live in.

Or what your denomination practices.

Or what traditions you've learned from whomever.

God wants to be worshiped in the way He has directed us to worship. But don't worry...it isn't all that complicated.

There are only two things—beyond salvation in Christ—the Bible says you must possess to enter into real worship. We need to know those two things, because there is a great deal of sound and activity in the contemporary church that may or may not be worship!

Now, some of the most clear direction we have on this subject in all of Scripture comes from the lips of the Lord Himself. As it happened, He was in the middle of a conversation with a prostitute by a well in a Samaritan village at high noon. But the *where* and *when* don't matter nearly as much as the *who* and *what*.

Let's drop in, for a moment, to the middle of their conversation. The Samaritan woman speaks first:

> Our fathers worshiped in this mountain; and ye say that in Jerusalem is the place where men ought to worship. Jesus saith unto her, Woman, believe me, the hour cometh, when ye shall neither in this mountain, nor yet at

Jerusalem, worship the Father. Ye worship ye know not what. We know what we worship; for salvation is of the Jews. But the hour cometh, and now is, when the true worshipers shall worship the Father in spirit and in truth; for the Father seeketh such to worship him. God is a Spirit; and they that worship him must worship him in spirit and in truth (John 4:20–24).

Now, Jesus Christ is the head of the New Testament church. He died for it. And if He says very clearly what *He* considers to be worship, don't you think you and I better know what it is? Because if you don't read the Instruction Manual and line up with God's intentions, you can be worshiping all you want, but you'll be leaving God right out of the equation.

True worship must be under the control of the Holy Spirit

That's the worshiping "in spirit" part. You have to be under the influence and direction of the Spirit of God with no unconfessed sins in your life. If that's the condition of your heart, you're already halfway there!

It's the atmosphere of your heart that counts... not the atmosphere of the building.

When it comes to entering into true worship, it's the atmosphere of your heart that counts...not the atmosphere of the building. When you attend a church that has a mixture of cultures and styles and preferences (the way, I believe, God intended it to be), your "perfect atmosphere for worship" may not happen very often—if ever! You may find yourself in a folding chair instead of a pew. You may be looking at a wrestling mat hanging on the wall of a converted gymnasium rather than through a stained-glass window with a soft, holy glow.

The externals may never line up the way you want them to.

The music may never send you into worshipful ecstasy. The pastor's tie may offend you, the color of the carpet may nauseate you, and the clapping and hand raising or *lack* of clapping and hand raising may annoy your sensibilities.

So what?

Allow me to repeat that, please. *So what?*

Those things are externals. Those things have very, very little to do with whether or not you are acceptably worshiping God. After all, who is the worship for? Is it for you? No, it is for the Lord, and He says, If you want to please ME with your worship, you must worship in spirit and in truth.

Your "perfect atmosphere for worship" may not happen very often—if ever!

How's your *spirit* when you walk through those doors on Sunday morning? If your spirit isn't right, all the stained glass and soft carpet and mellow music and comfortable pews in the world aren't going to help you worship. If your spirit is focused on yourself and your own preferences when you walk in, you may find yourself thinking, "Man, I can't stand that music. That's too much rock (or that's too much Bach). And look at those worship leaders up there. Those must be phony smiles. Why is she banging away on the tambourine? Why is that guy stiff as a two-by-four? When are we going to get a decent pianist?"

When you walk into the church building on Sunday morning, are you more concerned about what the music is going to be today or that your heart and mind are right with God, controlled and filled by His Holy Spirit?

You can get on the biggest high you've ever felt, you can have shivers running up and down your back and tears filling your eyes…but if your heart isn't right with the Spirit, it's just so much emotionalism. Or you can be quiet and reverent and soak up all the deep and solemn silence, but if your attitude toward others is proud and conceited, you are not a worshiper. You are wasting your time. You're not filled with the Holy Spirit, you are filled with yourself, and you cannot worship.

True worship must be in line with the truth

And what is that truth? It is the Word of God. You've got to be controlled by the Spirit—have your attitude and mind right toward others and toward God and yourself—and you have to be living a life obedient to the Scriptures. If you are walking in known disobedience to any biblical command, you cannot wor-

After all, who is the worship for? Is it for you? No!

ship. God will not receive it. He is looking for hearts; He is *seeking* men and women and children—who will worship Him with hearts filled with the Spirit and with lives obedient to His Word.

As an example, Jesus told His disciples: "Therefore if you bring your gift to the altar, and there remember that your brother has something against you, leave your gift there before the altar, and go your way. First be reconciled to your brother, and then come and offer your gift" (Matthew 5:23–24, NKJV).

First things first. Before you can worship, get your life back into alignment with the Word. If necessary, take care of business with your brother or your sister before you come to worship with God's people. If you have to, get up in the middle of the church service, walk out the door, and pick up the phone before you go any further. Worship in the Spirit. Worship in the truth. If you don't, you may be only fooling yourself. You may not be worshiping at all.

This is the New Testament model. This is what Jesus Christ says. And since He's the head of the church I'm going to go with Him.

"But traditionally," you say, "we always…"

I don't care about tradition. Tradition won't count for anything one second after you die. Jesus had it right when He told the Pharisees, "You have a fine way of setting aside the commands of God in order to observe your own traditions!" (Mark 7:9, NIV) We still do that, don't we?

The question is, are you worshiping in the Spirit and in the truth?

The Lord says to us, "Don't even bring your gift of praise to Me when you're bitter or resentful toward someone who's leading the music or because of the way someone's dressed or because of what someone said to you. Don't even *try* to worship Me, for how can you love Me whom you have not seen when you can't even love your brother or sister whom you have seen?"

Yes, music helps; it's a wonderful gift of God. Good acoustics, comfortable seating, and pleasant surroundings are all very nice, when they're available.

But God cares more about the atmosphere of the heart.

God cares more about obedience to His Word.

CONCLUSION

I magine that your grandparents had passed away and that you are responsible for taking their possessions out of storage and holding an estate sale. As you are sorting through some furniture stored in the dark corners of a basement, you come across what appears to be an old writing desk.

The thing is filthy—covered with dust and cobwebs and mouse droppings—and greasy from old cans of oil that have sat on top of it for years. Some years ago it had been painted with green paint, though now the paint is chipped and so grimy and weathered it's hard to tell what color it might have been.

You think to yourself, *Nobody would buy this old thing. I might as well chop it up and toss it in that big Dumpster out front.*

But then, as you're thinking about that, a memory comes back to you. In your mind's eye you can see your grandmother sitting at a desk something like this one when you were just a child. Only *that* desk had seemed—beautiful. You remember the nice wood grain. You remember how smooth it felt. You remember how the wood seemed to shine with a light of its own. You remember the shiny brass handles on the drawers.

Could this possibly be the same desk?

For some reason, you can't let go of that memory. You can't bring yourself to junk the desk. So you lift it into the back of your pickup and take it home to see what might be *under* all the grime and grease and old paint. Something in your heart tells you there's something beautiful under there.

The first job is just to wash the thing off in the backyard. Part of the time you're getting excited and saying to yourself, "This might be the piece of furniture I remember as a kid. This might be Grandma's writing desk!" But then when you look at what

Wouldn't it be wonderful to have it back the way it was?

shape the thing is in, you say, "Naw. Couldn't be. That was beautiful…and this thing's a wreck."

You know the steps you'll have to take, and it won't be easy. Stripper…then coarse sand paper…then medium sand paper…then fine sand paper…then steel wool…then…

But your curiosity drives you on, hour after hour, night after night. You can close your eyes and see your old grandma sitting there, writing letters. (And wasn't there some licorice she used to keep in that bottom drawer?)

But there is so much to strip away! Layer after sloppy layer of paint. Coat upon coat of old, yellowed varnish. Deep stains. This job could be discouraging…but the goal keeps you going. Wouldn't it be something to see that desk restored to its original beauty? Wouldn't it be wonderful to have it back the way it was?

That's a little word picture of what I've wanted to accomplish in this book. We've had the church of Jesus Christ with us for two thousand years now, and after studying the book of Acts, I've become convinced that what we see of the church throughout so much of our country today is a long, long way removed from the biblical pattern. In fact, it's barely recognizable as the original article.

Since those glorious days in the first century, the church has been painted over with men's traditions, chopped up into denominations, layered with false and unbiblical teaching, covered with the dust and stains of neglect, apathy, and outright sin.

Let's face it, the church isn't looking very good these days. We only see brief flashes of its beauty, shining through from time to time. Gradually the original grain has been lost, and each succeeding generation has added more gunk.

But the Word of God shows the original in all its craftsmanship. We don't have to guess at its beauty—it's there for all to see. We don't have to wonder about its power—Dr. Luke describes it in detail. And it's worth whatever we have to do to move today's church back to God's original intentions!

The good news is that the original can be ours, too.

The good news is that the original can be ours, too, if we go back to the Word of God with all our hearts and pursue the biblical pattern. This book was meant to be a small nudge in that direction. At the beginning, I asked the question, "Why doesn't the church today have the same power and impact on culture that the early church had?" In each following chapter, I tried to answer that question by returning to the teaching in the book of Acts...where the church was newly created.

It's like taking that writing desk out of the basement and stripping off those old layers—one by one—until we begin to see the magnificent pattern and grain and workmanship showing through.

Much of the church's beauty and glory has been hidden for years. It's time to rediscover its original simplicity and splendor.

But how do we do that?

We must seek the DAILY filling of God's Spirit

We have to strip that neglect away! Our casual, careless attitude about this crucial need is hiding the beauty and power of the church. We've got to get back in the Word and understand what it means to be filled and empowered—even intoxicated—with God's Spirit. Listen, we cannot accomplish *anything* of eternal significance apart from His day-by-day, moment-by-moment filling. Don't talk to me about how we've got it together in this program or that program! The church will not move forward by education...or marketing...or gimmicks...or committees...or conferences...or cultural sensitivity...or political action...or clever programs...or high-tech communication. If God's Spirit does not move us, then we do not move! We need to fall on our knees and cry out for His filling.

If God's Spirit does not move us, then we do not move!

We must saturate our lives in His Word

The sign gifts in the book of Acts always gathered a crowd, and the miracles grabbed the attention of the people, but the main event was the teaching of God's Word. It is the Word that shows us our sin and reveals our need of a Savior. It is the Word that declares Jesus Christ to be the Savior, the Son of God, and the King of kings and Lord of lords. It is the Word that shows us how to walk moment by moment in the Spirit of God. It is the Word that equips us for every situation we may face in this life. When we neglect the Word, the beauty of the church is hidden and the power to transform lives and even nations slips away from us.

We need to stop nibbling at the Word and start banqueting!

Signs and wonders and miracles have their place in God's scheme of things, but after all the smoke and fire have cleared away, it is the Word that gets God's business done. We need to quit tasting and nibbling at the Word and start banqueting! We need to scoot up to that training table and eat and eat and eat. Why? Because we're weak! We've been starving ourselves and don't even realize it.

We need fresh, Spirit-filled boldness in our witness

We've been wimps in the church! We've been afraid of our own shadows. Let's get busy. Let's quit hanging back. Let's remember that the church is an offensive force! I played defense in the NFL, but now, for the rest of my life, the Lord of the church has me on offense. And I like it! The Lord never intended us to huddle behind the "safe," protective walls of a building. The church isn't supposed to dig in and throw up defenses, it's supposed to *march!* The Lord called us to invade enemy territory and release the enemy's prisoners right from under his nose.

God doesn't want His people settling into a rut.

Do we expect to accomplish those things without a fight?

Do we expect the enemy to yield ground or surrender his prisoners easily? Scripture says that the gates of hell shall not prevail against us. Gates are defensive weapons. So what does that mean? It is hell that has to defend itself against the church on the move— but their walls can't stop us! We want to depopulate hell so that we can populate heaven.

We're marching out of our comfort zone into their comfort zone to make them get out of their comfort zone into someone else's comfort zone. That's the church! That's the power of the church. And the Holy Spirit will give us the boldness we need to accomplish the Father's plan.

Let's accept the fact that the church will never be comfortable

The Bible itself will strip this layer of old varnish away. The Word of God is sharper than a two-edged sword, and it penetrates this ungodly attitude and peels it away. When we live in the Word, guided by God's Spirit, it's going to keep us from getting comfortable. It's going to keep us on the edge of discomfort, because God doesn't want His people settling into a rut. We have no permanent city here; life is short, and there is no time to worry about personal comfort.

We know that when we are filled with the Spirit, saturated in the Word of God, and determined to be bold in our witness, we're going to encounter some uncomfortable situations. The Holy Spirit doesn't want us to settle into the comfort of mediocrity.

Let's stop fearing unpopularity and persecution

If we want to be like our Lord Jesus, then we should *expect* persecution. If we're going to do what is controversial we should expect controversy! Why are we so shocked that the world resists and mocks our values? Why are we so indignant that our leadership and the media don't embrace our priorities? The Lord *told* us it would be this way.

Complaining is the dark room of our life where we develop our negatives.

Let's just face the fact that not everyone is going to like us. They didn't like our Savior, either. As a matter of fact, they hated Him; and finally—when they had the chance to do what they really wanted to do—beat Him and abused Him and tortured Him and killed Him. So why should we win popularity contests with the same world that hated Jesus? Why should we cruise through life on a smooth path lined with roses? Let's remember again that the greatest blessing in all the world is to be disliked, shunned, ignored, mocked, taunted, and yes, even persecuted for the sake of Jesus' name. It is *blessed!*

God never intended us to look to our circumstances for comfort. Our comfort is from Him, the Father of compassion and God of all comfort. There's no comfort in going out to a world that's hostile to the gospel and rebellious to the rule of King Jesus. But don't let that opposition psyche you out. Can you imagine soldiers out on the front line saying, "Hey, I'm quitting this soldiering business because I'm being persecuted out here! Those guys are shooting at me! They're throwing things at me. They're trying to *hurt* me!"

Of course they are. If we expect anything less, we need to go back to God's Word for a refresher course. So let's eliminate that old fear of persecution that's covering up the true grain of the church.

We need to put murmuring far, far behind us

We're kind of a crazy army sometimes. We get so bogged down worrying about *where* we're marching and *how* we're marching that we've forgotten *why* we're marching. Complaining is simply the dark room of our life where we go to develop our negatives.

You tell me: What good comes of it? Does it solve anything? Does it even make you feel better? Does it help anyone else? The truth is, there's *nothing* good about it. And if there's nothing good about it, why are we doing it? Murmuring is the great, unchallenged sin of the church. But if we're filled with the Spirit, *He* will challenge it. God brought judgment on the Israelites after leaving Egypt because of their constant griping and whining. Do you think that He likes it any better today?

We need to strip our church of a murmuring mindset. And when we do, we will experience a great release of His power, flowing through us to a cynical world where complaining is just a way of life.

We need to use our spiritual gifts—with consistency and great joy!

People say, "Well, I just want to be fed." Or, "I'm just here to heal for a while." Or, "I just want to sit and listen."

Really? Why then did Christ call each of us into His body? His Word says that He wants us to serve, not to be served. To feed others, not just to be fed. To comfort and encourage, not just to be comforted and encouraged. God gave me my gift for the benefit of others! We need to have a Philippians 2 philosophy as believers when we look at our gifts—considering others as more important than ourselves. And when this happens—whoa! Watch out! There will not be any needs in the church, because before the church even hears about one, another member will have taken care of it.

Can you imagine the church taking care of one another's needs and not expecting someone else to do it? What a powerhouse! We'd have people *running* to get in the door. They'd be saying, "I saw what you did for my neighbor. And he told me he doesn't even have to pay it back! What's going on? What are you doing? What's this Jesus thing all about?"

When we strip off the old reluctance to use our gifts and start living our giftedness, the world will actually see the attributes of Jesus Christ. They'll see Him walking this earth again, ministering to needs, pulling hopeless men and women out of terrible darkness.

Because we're going to act like Christ.

We're going to talk like Christ.

We're going to reveal their wrongs like Christ.

We're going to bring them into the kingdom like Christ.

And we're going to love like Christ, with a loyal, faithful, self-sacrificing love that can penetrate even hardened hearts.

We need to courageously pursue church discipline and mutual accountability

Following the deaths of Ananias and Sapphira in Acts 5, Scripture says that "great fear came upon all the church, and upon as many as heard these things." Can you imagine a disciplined church where people fear the awesomeness of God and have a burning desire for personal purity? Can you imagine a church where people know that leadership will hold them accountable to walk with Christ, just as they hold their leadership to the same standards? Where brothers and sisters in Christ hold each other to high standards of conduct and service?

Accountability makes me check my speedometer ...and my lifestyle.

If you can't imagine it, it may be because you've never seen it! But that was our Lord's intention for His church.

Fear of sin! Love of righteousness!

God says in Romans 13 that He only gave government for those who do wrong. Discipline isn't for those who do right; it is for those who do wrong. I call it "Reverend Government." And if you don't think it works, watch what happens next time a policeman pulls up behind you on the interstate. He doesn't even need to turn his blue light on; his very *presence* makes you check your speedometer!

What does accountability do? It makes me check my speedometer. It makes me check my lifestyle. It tells me: Man, I'd better check how I'm doing, how I'm driving, how I'm talking, how I'm acting, where I am, what I'm watching, how I'm working, where I'm spending my time.

Oh, but not us. We're afraid of accountability. We're afraid of offending someone. We think we're "too mature" to be held accountable. Do you think "mature" people shouldn't need accountability? Then you'd better talk to King David. If he'd had a little of it on the night he went walking on the palace roof, history would have been changed.

We need to wholeheartedly embrace the biblical pattern for the church

We need to remove the years of varnish of doing it our own way, doing it the traditional way, doing it the denominational way, doing it the way I like it, doing it the way that makes me comfortable. You can't see the beautiful wood grain of the original church if you've painted over it with your own preferences!

There is a better way.

It's in the Book.

And when God's work is done by God's people in God's way, empowered by God's mighty, indwelling Spirit, look out, Jack!

We will be a force to be reckoned with!